3 - 18 - 76

Please Get Off the Seesaw Slowly

Please Get Off the Seesaw Slowly

NORMA WILLIAMSON

Fleming H. Revell Company
Old Tappan, New Jersey

Library of Congress Cataloging in Publication Data

Williamson, Norma.
    Please get off the seesaw slowly.

    1. Women—Conduct of life. 2. Women—Religious life. I. Title.
BJ1610.W54   242′.6′33   75–4999
ISBN 0–8007–0738–9

TO Cecil without whose relentless encouragement
the first word would never have been written
—and without whom there wouldn't be much
in my life to write about anyway.

Contents

Foreword by Perry Tanksley

Muddling Through

When Perfume Won't Work

Pigtails and Other Problems

Loosen Your Tension and Operate in a Normal Manner

Foreword

Cast thy bread upon the waters: for thou shalt find it after many days.

Ecclesiastes 11:1

Someone paraphrased that Scripture verse: "Cast your bread upon the waters and after many days it will return unto you—buttered, with jam on it, and marked WITH LOVE!"

Norma Williamson is the kind who can't wait for the butter, jam, and love. In this faith-lifting volume *Please Get Off the Seesaw Slowly* she is casting her bread with liberal amounts of the three other ingredients. And I found the bread goes down easily with all the butter and jam and love she includes in these lines.

Some books I do not throw aside lightly. I throw them with great force! *Please Get Off the Seesaw Slowly* was not one of them. I read these pages and found enough pathos to make me cry, enough wit to make me laugh, and enough openness and honesty to cast a searchlight on my own needy soul. Because Norma has said *yes* to Life, her contagious enthusiasm shines brightly from this testament of faith. My prayer for this book is that it will find its way into every home where this language is spoken.

PERRY TANKSLEY

Acknowledgments

There are two Christian gentlemen to whom I must acknowledge a great debt. Roy Lawrence, editor of the *Mississippi United Methodist Advocate*, accepted with kindness and enthusiasm the first material I submitted to him and has let me write a biweekly column for him since 1972. Some of the material in this book has previously appeared in that column, and it is included here with Roy's permission.

Perry Tanksley, whose books are well known to many, first put me in touch with Fleming H. Revell Company. His encouragement and guidance have been invaluable. I cannot repay him; I simply acknowledge the debt.

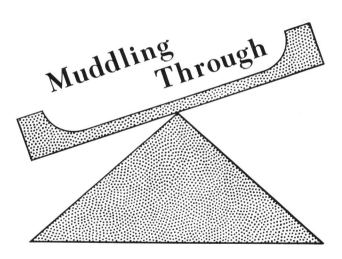
Muddling Through

1
Some Days Life is Just Great!

When our teen-ager spends half an hour reading *Mother Goose* to his little brothers with such gestures and expression that any rendition I subsequently give it will be dull by comparison;

When my daughter brings me breakfast in bed only an hour after I've dropped medicine into her aching ear;

When my four-year-old patiently takes his brother of two by the hand and leads him safely around the floor furnace;

When one brother gives up a cherished toy because the other is crying for it;

When my husband comes in, takes one look at my face, and says, "Let's eat out tonight."

Then I know that great are my blessings and many to be counted. And I wouldn't swap this noisy, boisterous household for all the peace and quiet in the world.

2
Save Your Breath

Any mother-in-the-making soon learns that there are certain things which, left unsaid, have exactly as much effect as if they were spoken. Here are a few things I have stopped saying in order to conserve energy:

"If you climb any higher up that tree, you're liable to fall." *(Energy conserved is used to pick up the pieces and call the doctor.)*

"If you would zip your zippers and turn your socks when you take them off, it would take you only a split second and it would save me several minutes of laundry time, since I have to do it for six people." *(Energy conserved is used for zipping up zippers and turning socks.)*

"If you don't stop giving your sister a hard time, I am going to be forced to paddle you." *(Energy conserved is used for paddling.)*

"If you insist on bringing the kitten inside, someone is going to have a mess to clean up." *(Energy conserved is used to clean floor.)*

"If you'll wait a second, I'll help you pour that milk." *(Energy conserved. . . .)*

Actually, I have concluded that there is no point at all in ever beginning a sentence with "If . . ." when you're talking to a child. There is that built into each of us (worked out of some around the age of thirty, and out of some, never) which springs into life or bursts into flame at the sound of *if.* It is the adventurous quality, the pioneer spirit, the same urge which drove our forefathers away from the relatively civilized Eastern shores across the Mississippi, over the mountains, and through the desert on to the Golden West. It is the same spirit which has put man on the moon. It is the same drive that motivated Admiral Byrd, Magellan, and Hernando de Soto. Without it we would not have electric lights, steamboats, or permanent waves. We would be still sweeping our floors with shuck brooms, mowing the grass by means of hungry sheep, and getting to the next town on foot.

To *if* a proposition to a child is to insure that it will be attempted if you fear it and ignored if you favor it. Would you dare your child to do something? Of course not. Then don't tantalize him with *if* either.

You might as well save your breath!

3
I Have Discovered Empirically That the Family Hazards Increase Exponentially With the Advent of Each Child
or
There Are Too Many People Around Here!

When my first two children were small, I used to change the "Old Woman Who Lived in a Shoe" nursery rhyme to conclude "And she *kissed* them all soundly. . . ." By the time numbers three and four came along, that rhyme was back where it started, and the poor, harassed mother, ". . . whipped them all soundly and put them to bed" as any normal mother would do after seeing to a dozen or so children all day. I began to wonder whether I had too many children myself when I gave medicine twice to the same child and left a second one entirely undosed. (Of course, I should have suspected something when the double-dosed one howled like a banshee and the other ordinarily noisy one betook himself discreetly away.)

There was a time when, if one child protested, "But you never *told* me!" I could reply firmly and with assurance, "Oh, yes, I did!" But now I am never quite sure whether I did, indeed, tell that one, or another one, or just thought about it. (Somehow I think they suspect this.)

I understand that when someone asked Susanna Wesley why she gave the same instructions nineteen times, she replied, "Why, because eighteen are not enough," the implication being that if the child heard it often enough it would make an effective imprint. But *I* know better than that—*I* know that she said a thing nineteen times to be sure the right child heard it.

I would be surprised to find any large family (loosely defined as a family with more than one child) whose children had acceptable table manners. For example, I really think it is not only impolite but tends to be a little untidy to talk with one's mouth full. But even our youngest has learned that when a quiet moment comes, if he wants it he'd better grab it, because if he takes time to chew and swallow, someone else will have the floor. At our table, empty mouth and empty moment never coincide.

I am thinking seriously of petitioning the proper authorities for a staggered schedule among the schools. The traffic jam in our bathrooms on school mornings is something to behold and when the last kindergartner (who leaves the house thirty minutes after the others and is never allowed inside a bathroom before eight A.M. for any reason) enters regular school, the situation can only get worse.

We decided this progressive country had come full circle in convenience when our youngest marched into the family room one morning, dropped into a chair, and made this disgruntled announcement: "I'm just going to build me a bathroom outside; the ones in this house are always full!"

4
A Father Is a Necessary Thing

I am so glad God made fathers!

There are some things mothers can't do worth a hoot. I worked on that bicycle chain for nearly half an hour, urged on with "Daddy did it last time quick as a minute!" I couldn't run fast enough to help at all the day we took the training wheels off the bike. My leg-horsie is extremely short-winded, and my kites never do fly.

Fathers can drive straighter nails and wield a neater paintbrush than mothers can. They can even put on Band-Aids better, especially if they've been out of town for a few days. They tell more exciting yarns and funnier jokes; they find the best places to hide. And the dogs on the next block don't bark nearly so fiercely when Dad is walking with us.

The sky is bluer, the flowers are prettier, and the birds sing sweeter when Daddy is at home. Mother is more relaxed and patient, daughters are gentler, and boys are braver. The supper table becomes a banquet, and a walk around the block takes on the lure of a pirate's adventure.

A family is indeed incomplete without a father. Every person feels the emptiness with a special and individual pang. What a wise and loving Father we have to have planned for His children as He did!

5
Ten Things You Might As Well Not Do Anyway

Ten things you might as well not do because they're not going to affect the situation one whit anyway:

Serve roast beef and rice and gravy and chocolate pie the day the bank statement comes in.

Remind a small boy that he has nine toes that aren't sore.

Assure your offspring that it isn't absolutely necessary to address you as "honorable and aged mother."

Try to get to the root of any sibling squabble.

Explain to a teen-ager that it doesn't constitute hypocrisy to offer a polite excuse when declining a party invitation.

Ask anybody under twenty to close the door quietly.

Mop the kitchen floor on a rainy summer day.

Instruct an older brother not to yell at, threaten, tease, or otherwise harass his younger sister.

Counsel said sister not to react to said harassment either verbally or by facial expression.

Resolve not to lose your perspective, your sense of humor, or your sanity during any given ordinary family occurrence.

6
A Road Map I Can Follow

Bathing a small boy is like navigating uncharted territory. It's the hardest job I do on an ordinary day, and it comes when I have the least reserve of energy to put forth. I never could understand mothers who bathe their small children in the mornings—either they don't have normally dirty children or they change their sheets every day.

Actually the hardest part of the job is the first: getting him into the tub. You start with his face and, if you're lucky, you get at least two swipes before he howls: "You got soap in my eyes!" or, "My dears ain't 'irty!" On to the neck, and it's, "Quit choking me!" and down to the hands where, "You're peelin' my fingernails off!" Back and tummy offer a little respite: no convolutions where the crafty dirt can hide from you, no smarting membranes, relatively few scratches and mosquito bites—just nice, smooth planes where the suds can start at the top and slide downwards while you watch the color darken.

Legs and feet are something else. There are more hazards per square inch on the lower extremities of a small boy than on the heights of Everest. And, as on the mountaintop, the risk varies with the season. Winter is the easiest of all (praise heaven for thick jeans), spring and fall are fair-to-middling, but summer brings an unqualified nightmare. The toes require the tenderest, most careful treatment of all, and they never fail to create in me an urge to grab the dog brush and the steel wool.

Finally, you coax him out, scrub him down with the towel (taking advantage of every excuse for a hug), and get him into his pjs. Then you sit down on the floor and, with him snuggling inside one arm and his brother inside the other, you start the story.

And then you remember why you had him after all.

7
Wishes I Have Made

To eat an Oreo cooky with the filling still in it.

To turn a doorknob and not have to wash sticky whatever off my hands.

To get more than two swallows while the coffee is still hot.

To spend ten minutes behind a closed door without hearing a crash and/or a wail.

To sleep all night through and wake to find every bed in the house dry.

To vacuum the floor without a couple of passengers on the choo-train.

To eat a meal with no incident of spilled milk or juice or both.

To tie a pair of shoelaces and expect them to stay that way at least an hour.

To do the laundry or cook a meal or cut out a garment or perform any other small- to middle-sized job from start to finish without being sidetracked in midstream.

To have the grace to remember that when all these other wishes come true—it's going to be mighty quiet and lonely around here.

8
Two: Trouble and Triumph

A two-year-old is one who listens to a recitation of "Humpty Dumpty," and then remarks, "They could, too!" A two-year-old will say no to an ice cream cone, a walk in the park, or a new puppy—if his mother suggests it. And the surest way to get him to do something is to tell him not to. Two will insist, "I can!" when you are sure the task is much too complicated for him, and state just as emphatically, "I can't!" when you know perfectly well he certainly could if he just would.

Two puts more joy into a "Hi, doggie!" than most of us Christians generate for "Alleluia! Christ is risen!" A moonstruck swain never offered his love a rose with purer or more complete devotion than does a two-year-old when he brings his mother a clover blossom. A two-year-old can put an unwanted extra ice cube in the middle of your dinner plate with all the innocence of infancy, but there lurks an imp in his eye all the same.

Two will entertain himself for long stretches of time, playing the part of each character in his fantasy world. At other times, all forty-nine verses of his day-long dirge begin with "I don't have nuffin' to do." He spends minutes admiring himself in the mirror with the sort of unselfconscious detachment that it is a pity we women don't have. Two can threaten your sanity and stretch your patience to a thin thread, and then restore your balance with four words, "I love you, Mama."

My youngest just turned three. I shall miss the Terrible Twos.

9
Some Things I Hope I Never Forget

The feel of my toddler's right arm around my waist while his left hand wreaks havoc with my piano playing;

The sound of his voice singing "Feelin' Groovy" as he sways back and forth precariously—standing on the arm of the rocking chair;

The sight of my teen-ager on the floor romping with his two little brothers—the sound of their shrieks and laughter;

The conversations with my daughter as she shares her growing Christian convictions with me;

The expression on my husband's face when he discovers one of his sons enjoying something he himself likes to do;

The Winnie-the-Pooh growl of a small child's voice first thing every morning;

The giggling of the two little ones as they perpetrate some innocent mischief against an older one;

The warmth and rapport and the indefinable "special" feeling when we rev up the fireplace for the first time in the fall;

The sights, sounds, and smells at Thanksgiving, Christmas, Sunday dinner, Grandpa's birthday, or any other occasion that brings us all together.

10
Train Up a Child

The Bible says, "Train up a child in the way he should go, and when he is old, he will not depart from it" (Proverbs 22:6). I'm in there trying; verily, I am doing my dead level best, but sometimes I wish these children would hurry up and get old so they will stop departing.

There are times when I'm pretty sure the training is not taking at all, as witness one particular night when I was on my knees leading the two little boys' prayers (you do understand that my leading doesn't necessarily mean anyone was following!). As a matter of fact, one of them climbed on my back to ride horsie and the prayer wafted upwards with a pronounced rhythm: *"Now* I *lay* me *down* to *sleep. . . ."* A relative gave these same two boys some felt take-apart men, the parts of which buttoned together ingeniously and the purpose of which was to keep tots still during church services. One child worked diligently and in reasonable quiet until the last button, then exclaimed with glee, "Hoo-ee! That man has rabbit ears!"

Many have been the times when I have had to turn a preschooler over to a parishioner for safekeeping while I was at the organ and his dad was in the pulpit. One child must have been nearly four at the time he eluded his keeper, slipped quietly up into the choir loft, and, spotting me on the opposite side of the organ, proceeded to cross over to me, "playing" on every single pedal on the bass scale while I struggled frantically to reach him. Another was a little less than hospitable when during his first visit to "real" church at the age of three, some strangers sat down on the opposite end of our pew, and he announced in an indignant stage whisper, "Somebody else is sitting on our chair!"

Well, the promise is there. And whether it means stifling a

snort of laughter at the fervent plea, "Please bless Uncle Bob's pigs," or satisfying the curiosity expressed during a sermon, "Why is that man yelling so loud?" we have our work cut out for us. Ours is to do the training: the pruning, weeding, and cultivating, or whatever is required. The Lord will surely give the growth and bring forth fruit in due time.

11
It's Not the Real Thing

On two or three occasions in my life I have taken employment outside the home for a period of time. During seminary days I worked in the dean's office and as a church secretary; after I received my degree, I taught school briefly (long enough, theoretically, to put back into the family kitty what I had taken out to finance my education). But I have never worked harder to earn less money than on those occasions when I have served as a substitute teacher.

Actually, substitute teaching comes under the heading of community service. The remuneration—no matter what the amount—is not pay for services rendered. There is not enough money in any state's treasury to compensate its substitute teachers adequately. The pay just helps ease the pain a little.

The task is difficult enough when you're in your own field. To walk into a classroom with no advance preparation, pick up another's plan, and proceed to lecture or demonstrate from it is enough to set the most stalwart soul a-tremble. But to presume to do it in a subject area where (if the truth be known) you know less than the students is roughly akin to finding yourself at the controls of a plane for the first time. The take-off is uncertain, the ride full of hazards, and the landing a severe let-down.

Nothing can brighten a student's day like unexpectedly finding a substitute in the teacher's chair. An ordinarily unimaginative and uncommunicative scholar can come to life and lead a witty discussion on everything in the encyclopedia in order to keep the teacher off the subject. The dullest wit in the room never lacks for words when a substitute is standing in the gap. Indeed, if all the effort expended to avoid the subject were directed toward mastering it, the regular teacher would find a roomful of geniuses on her return.

While I have never discovered a tack in my chair nor a snake
in my desk (as have certain of my fellow sufferers), I read the
message from these red-herring specialists loud and clear: AS A
BABY-SITTER FOR OUR DAY-LONG PARTY, WE WELCOME YOU.
JUST DON'T BOTHER US WITH ANY SERIOUS SCHOOL STUFF,
PLEASE.

12
Scene I, Scene II

Wash the windows, mop the floors;
  Wax the tables, scrub the doors;
Clean the children, threaten same;
  Polish silver, bake the ham.
Kitchen shining, pets all banished;
  Music playing, toys vanished.
    TELEPHONE: *So sorry, dear; last minute change*
              in plans prevents our coming!
All that flutter! For nothing!

Kitchen messy, baby crying;
  Children yelling, Mother sighing;
Puppy barking, Dad a-frown;
  Meat too cold, rolls too brown.
Tables dusty, floors unvarnished;
  Linens wrinkled, silver tarnished.
    DOORBELL: *Surprise! Surprise! We thought we'd*
             come and spend a day or two with you!
All that clutter! Oh, help!

13
Alone in a Crowd

When we were first married, we lived on a large university campus in what amounted to an apartment dormitory, three stories tall with sixteen apartments on each floor. Those apartments were furnished with the minimal necessities (some, such as the stove and refrigerator, in miniature). There we experienced the next thing to communal living. If we were invited to a meal with another couple, it was understood that we were to take along our own ice trays and dining chairs. (Years later when a parishioner called to ask us out and I started out the door with my newspaper-wrapped bundle under my arm, my husband asked, "Why are you taking the ice trays?")

Resourceful husbands added all manner of accoutrements to make those tiny apartments livable—not with consistent success. One friend of mine had a shelf of diminishing width attached to her kitchen door, which was also the only exit. On it she kept her canisters of sugar, flour, and the like—until the day her husband left in a huff and slammed the door behind him, depositing on the kitchen floor a small mountain of sugar, flour, rice, and coffee. I had hung a series of frying pans on my own door but decided to remove them when, during someone's too hasty exit, one was jarred loose and bounced across the floor, the pan going in one direction and its handle in another.

For most of us, the Murphy beds which folded up into the wall were our only sleeping facilities (some time later, we bought a couch for twelve dollars and sold it after eighteen months' use for five). But those of us who couldn't afford hotel arrangements for visiting parents and other relatives worked out a swap system with each other. When we received notice of an impending visit, it remained only to check around and find a couple who would be going home the same weekend, and that was that.

There was one time when a friend's couch saved me from a miserable night. Early in our marriage, my husband had to go out of town for a week. As I was working as well as attending classes, I had to remain behind. While I didn't look forward to being alone, it really didn't occur to me that with roughly a hundred other people in the building (all acquaintances if not friends) I would be frightened at night. But I had gone from sisters to college roommate to husband and had never, up to that point, slept in a room alone. As twilight gave way to darkness that first day my apprehension rose. I ate my solitary meal, finished my assignments, did all my little night things, and crawled into bed preparing to read myself to sleep. If there is anything worse to a lone woman at night than a house with all kinds of creaks and noises, it is a house full of a hundred people with no noise at all. At midnight I gave up.

I made a mental inventory of friends I considered close enough to invite myself to spend the night with, eliminated from those the ones who didn't have a couch, and was left with two names. Bundling up in a robe, I let myself out the front door and, with pounding heart, surveyed the windows to determine whether one of the two still had a light burning. Luck was with me.

My light tap brought a surprised and sleepy seminarian to the door. By this time completely unnerved, I blinked back tears and asked,

"Bob, may I spend the night with you and Doris?"

"Why? What's up?"

I had to laugh as he glanced up and down the hall in disbelief and amazement—looking, I realized, for my husband. Satisfied with my explanation that an absent husband—not an angry one —was the source of my unhappiness, the two of them took me in and settled me down for what remained of the night.

But I still don't like sleeping in a house alone. And if my husband is still traveling when all these children grow up, I plan to invest in several very large, very noisy clocks.

14
Please Go Away and Let Me Sleep

They say that opposites attract, and nowhere is there a clearer case in point than in my own marriage. My husband is naturally athletic, well coordinated, even graceful in motion. He is an excellent swimmer, plays a passable, though infrequent, game of golf, is a good shot and a tireless jogger. I sport a variety of bruises gained from bumping into the furniture, break more dishes than our four-year-old, and get the bulk of my exercise from opening and refolding the newspaper. To his utter disgust, I squeeze the toothpaste tube in the middle; he is the sort of person who buys a key to roll the tube up on. He is a TV watcher; I am a reader. He is socially at ease in a crowd of any size, while I—if I had my druthers—would take my friends in twos and threes.

But nowhere is this divergence more evident than in our sleeping and waking habits. My husband is an early riser—voluntarily so. He is not content to rise early; he has to do it in a good mood, wide-awake the instant he touches feet to floor. Nobody but another sleepy-headed bride can understand the shock and dismay that were mine when, early on the second day of our marriage, I was faced with this heretofore unknown fact of his existence. The vista of years stretched out before me: morning after morning when I would be rudely awakened by the opening and closing of drawers, the rush of running water, the unearthly *scritch* of clothes hangers being pushed along the rod in the closet. I nestled down under the covers and put my face between the pillows in an effort to recapture my dreams. At that moment, "Old Man River" issued from the confines of the bathroom in a warm, rolling baritone. Shortly, the tempo picked up considerably and the melody moved into a higher key signaling (I was to learn later) the switch from warm to cold water.

Some time later, in a moment of unwifely disloyalty, I was bemoaning my fate to a friend.

"My dear," she said to me, "have you forgotten that my apartment is directly over yours? I have just been thanking my lucky stars that anyone who can sing that loud at that unearthly hour of the morning can at least sing on key!"

15
Caution: *Driver Asleep*

My husband is a much better driver than I am. I know this is true because if I drove thirty thousand miles a year the way he drives, I'd have been dead a long time ago.

As we were tooling along the highway one sunny summer afternoon our four-year-old sat on my lap prattling along with one of his interminable monologues. "Mama, you know what I'm going to do when we get home? I'm going to teach Boots to sit up and shake my hand. Mama, yesterday I almost caught a butterfly with my own fingers. *Mama, did you know Daddy can drive a car with his eyes closed?*"

And this was no isolated incident. Only the watchful eyes of a merciful God and a few thousand fellow drivers have preserved him alive and whole. He has tried every remedy under the sun to keep himself alert behind the wheel: letting the radio blare at full volume, chewing gum, nibbling on candy bars, listening to sermons on the tape recorder (I could have told him that wouldn't have the desired effect), even, to my utter and very vocal horror, smoking cigars. I am glad to say this last effort, being as hard on his stomach as it was on my nose, was exceedingly short-lived.

If his thoughts are sufficiently tangled or deep, he can sit all the way through one green light and well into the second before irate horns behind him arouse him to move on. On the other hand, he has been known to sail through a red light without ever knowing it was there. Somewhere around the Southeast, there are doubtless several dozen citizens who, on one day or another, arrived home safe if trembling to make a raid on the aspirin bottle before relating to their wives tales of horror about an absent-minded hazard driving around in a brown sedan who had just added several streaks of white to their own heads.

There is one thing to his credit: He never seems annoyed when I—or some other family member—call his attention to a traffic signal or an oncoming car. All of us have learned to keep a sharp vigil. And I have begun the practice of fortifying him with several cups of coffee before travel time, especially if we plan to have an extra passenger. I'm sure it must be a little unnerving to the uninitiated to hear without preamble: "Wake up, Daddy; we're coming to a curve."

16
To Keep or Not to Keep

Around our house we have two kinds of people: savers and throwers-away. My husband is a saver. I am not. He growls that if I had my way the house would be stripped clean of everything but the bare necessities of living—and a one-day supply of that. I contend that if we kept everything he wanted to keep we would now be living on the rooftop, having used up all the space inside the house for storing the things we "might need someday." We have enough plastic bottles to float a battleship, newspapers sufficient to line a football field, and a ball of twine that I can't even pick up any more.

I have never gone so far as to give his last year's suit to the Goodwill people, but I have, over the years, developed a little system that allows me walking space in each room. Perfecting this system was no simple process; it has taken years to evolve. Many are the times I have dusted around, cleaned under, and rearranged some of his stores to the point that finally, in exasperation, I threw them out only to have him inquire within a day or two,

"Sweetheart, have you seen that little flat box I was saving?"

So I have learned to be methodical about my clearing-house activities. I stick something out of sight in a brown paper bag, and if he doesn't ask for it within a reasonable time—say a year or two or three—I throw it away, being very careful not to look inside the bag. Then the next day, when he asks, "Have you seen . . . ?" I can truthfully say, "No, I'm afraid not."

On one particular day I stood on a chair discarding and reorganizing the medical supplies on the top shelf of the hall closet. As fast as I dropped certain outdated items into the wastebasket beside the chair he rescued them.

"How come you're throwing this throat spray away?" he demanded indignantly. "It's still good." And he demonstrated with a cloud of mist directed toward me. I couldn't even see him through the haze.

"You can't use that old stuff," I protested. "Why, it'll peel your tongue."

Finally realizing that as long as he stayed around I would get nowhere, I suggested in no uncertain terms,

"Why don't you get out of here and let me get my work done?"

Our three-year-old, who had observed this little interchange in growing distress, grabbed her father by the leg and wailed,

"Please don't throw my daddy away, Mommy. We can't get another one of him!"

And, oh, she was so right!

17
Not Many Dull Moments

When my husband was in seminary, I worked as a secretary in the dean's office. That experience was an education in itself. I developed a better-than-nodding acquaintance with some gracious and brilliant gentlemen whom I would probably never have met otherwise. One student I remember was a retired college mathematics professor who was beginning a new career in the ministry. He was an engaging fellow and one of the most industrious and diligent among the students. I thought that, though his ministry would be shorter than most, it would be fruitful and effective since he would bring to it at the outset a balance and maturity others could gain in the only way he had —through experience.

There were several foreigners among the student body and a few on the faculty. One Scotsman I came to love had a *Mc* name, and on occasion when he dictated a letter to me he referred to his wife as "Mrs. McNut." (I listened for him to refer to himself as "Professor McNut," but, strangely, he never did.) It never failed to startle me when a professor who, in my mind, was supposed to be staid and sedate and dignified cracked a joke or created a pun. The Hebrew professor had a habit of referring to students who did not take his course as "poor, benighted brethren." At the annual student banquet one year, the menu was printed in Hebrew on one side and, on the other, for the sake of the "poor, benighted brethren"—and presumably the guests—it appeared in English.

Every day in that office brought a new experience. Once a delivery man appeared at the door with a huge crate in his arms.

"I'm here with the rabbits, ma'am," he announced.

"Rabbits? What rabbits?" I inquired.

"I don't know, ma'am. Somebody ordered 'em and I was told to bring them here."

"Are you sure? What would we do with rabbits?" I stammered.

He shuffled his feet. Then,

"What do they do here?" he wanted to know.

"They teach."

"But what do they teach?" he pursued.

"Well, they teach preaching."

A glance at the label on the crate about this time indicated that the rabbits were destined for the biology building next door, and I directed him there without bothering to explain the difference in departments. As he turned toward the door, he muttered, not entirely under his breath,

"Teachin' preachin', wantin' rabbits! What kind of a place *is* this?"

18
Don't Do It My Way

Just in case I am ever invited to teach it, I have prepared a syllabus for a course entitled *How Not to Be a Counselor at Camp*. I am eminently well qualified to give it, though I can point with pride to no study or research into the subject. I learned it *all by myself*.

The first thing you don't do is say to the recruiter, "If you cannot find anyone else, I'll help you." That kind of remark puts an end to any further search for personnel, no matter whether you're talking about singing in the choir, soliciting for community funds, or counseling at junior camp. The next thing you don't do is remain whole and in good health right up to the day the camp opens. Believe me, if you're going to be broken down and old before your time, you might as well admit to it before you put in such a strenuous week as shepherding six lively little girls twenty-four hours a day.

If, having failed in the first points, you find yourself on the lists and at the starting point, you might as well resolve to do the best you can. So one thing you must refuse to do at the outset (unless you are a professional athlete) is take the swimming test. At the time of my downfall—an expression more apt than you might think—I had not been in the water for two years, and I was the only person from my cabin to fail the test. As every camp has a qualified lifeguard anyway, there's no need to expose your weakness to your charges on the very first day—they'll discover it soon enough.

At my particular place of experience, the custom is for the counselor to sit at the head of the table during meals and serve all the plates, her own last. Under no circumstances should you follow this practice. There is no limit to the amount of food healthy young females can stow away, and the speed with which they can do it is not to be believed. I no sooner got the last plate filled and passed than the first one was back in my hands empty, forwarded by a sprite whose lean and hungry look would melt the heart of a Tartar.

I lost seven pounds and three towels that week but I gained six fast friends. I do believe it was worth it after all!

19
H-E-L-P *Spells Trouble*

I tell you it is disconcerting to be married to a man who can do everything I can do faster and better. I don't refer to such things as loosening stubborn jar lids and reaching tall cabinets. Those are the tasks that any prudent wife asks her husband to do for her. After all, we don't want them to think we could get along without them, do we? Nor do I allude to special areas in which he may excel by reason of natural talent. Everyone is simply not equipped with the same abilities, and it is no threat to me that this is so. For example, my husband is a superb public speaker, and the larger the crowd the more eloquently he holds forth; I, on the other hand, have difficulty forming a complete sentence if all my children are listening to me at the same time. (Wouldn't you quail before four pairs of eyes riveted on you in everything from patient resignation to the kind of scrutiny that makes you wonder if your nose is smudged?)

In such areas as those where he is naturally superior, I yield gracefully. But to discover that he outclasses me at things I'm supposed to excel in is nothing short of demoralizing. I have never worried that he would go hungry during my annual treks to my parents' home; he cooks a lot of things as well as I do. When a new baby comes or on those rare occasions when I have succumbed to illness and taken to my bed, he proves to be more efficient with the laundry and housekeeping than I am. It's enough to make me sick all over again.

At such times when my morale takes a nose dive and I suspect him of marrying me because a preacher looks more dignified with a wife than without, I wilt in shame until I remember that, in one area at least, he is helpless as a kindergartner. He could not write a sermon or a letter without help because he is one of those individuals who cannot spell well enough to find a word in the dictionary. So when he patiently waves me aside, cleans my sticky goo off the waffle iron, and turns out a serving of golden, crisp perfection, I wither him with *"Hah!* Spell *accommodate!"*

It works every time.

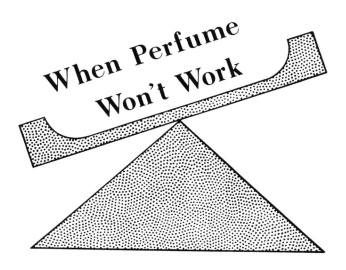

1
Perfume—or Prayer?

O, Father, I'm blue this morning. My tail feathers are drooping in the dust. I've already gone through all my old tricks: I've perfumed myself, made my face up, done my hair nicely; I'm even wearing this new red sweater. What's wrong? Why haven't I perked up?

I don't really have to ask You that, Lord. Down inside myself I know why, because down inside me is where the trouble is. The disease isn't superficial; therefore, superficial remedies don't help.

I'm hurting inside, Lord, because I've been turning my back on the light. Away from the light I miss the warmth, and I'm cold—cold, and uncertain, and fearful. I don't like this shuddering, vague apprehension—this "something is wrong, but I don't know what" feeling. I want to be back where I've been before: in the middle of Your light and Your love.

I know when I wandered away, Lord. I was in that crowd and I wanted to say something startling and memorable, and it was neither; it was silly and cheap. I'm ashamed of that; I'm sorry I loosed my tongue. I say I belong to You; forgive me for shaming You. And then I wanted something that wasn't mine, Lord. I wanted it, and I thought about how it would be to have it, and I let my mind dwell on it with envy and covetousness. And the longer I dwelt, the dimmer the light became.

Turn me in the right direction, Lord. Let the heat of Your holy light penetrate my cold and envious mind, purge my unrighteous heart, and purify my careless and wicked tongue. Let me know again the joy and confidence of being wholly Yours.

I am Yours; I do love You. Thank You for reminding me; thank You for forgiving me; thank You for promising to keep me!

Thanks, too, Lord, for perking me up. It's a great day!

2
Too Much?

Lord, you know I am just sick to death of economizing. We're all tired of beans and cheese, and I don't want to squeeze a third cup of tea out of that soggy teabag. Psychologically, it *does* something to me to put the cold, limp thing in my cup. And I want a new suit, not just a new scarf to perk up an old one. In fact, I'd really appreciate a whole new wardrobe, skin-out.

The children could use some shoes, too. And just once in a great while, I'd like to throw caution to the breeze and splurge on a night out—dinner—a movie—the works. I wish we could spend just one month without having to say to some request, "No, we can't afford it."

Am I asking too much, Lord? New clothes, plenty of food in the pantry, funds for recreation? Yes, I am. I know better than that. Here I sit in my warm bedroom, bare feet on carpeted floor, dinner easily prepared and cooking now in my automatic oven. I ought to be ashamed of myself. I *am* ashamed of myself. We've never needed—*really* needed—a single thing that You didn't provide for us. I am grateful, Lord.

I passed those houses between here and school yesterday— houses that don't have central heating, automatic stoves, some of them even without plumbing. And I read the paper. I know there are people somewhere in the world who would be so happy to have just beans and cheese—who would feel fortunate to have a blanket to wrap up in against the chill of an unheated house.

I expect I have a counterpart somewhere, Lord, who will put her children to bed tonight and then lie down herself with the knowledge that they are hungry and cold and sick. And she can't get up tomorrow to call the doctor because there is no doctor to call—and no money to pay him if he were there. She will dress them in too-tight coats and too-short pants and in cold, stiff shoes without socks. She will wipe a runny nose with a shirt tail, and then hug a little one close to her with a mute prayer that love will make up for warmth and food and clothes.

Yes, Lord, I certainly ask too much. Forgive me. Forgive me.

3
It's Been a Long Day

Oh, Lord, I'm sorry to come complaining again, but I'm tired of being the family sponge. I've soaked up all the gripes and complaints and bickering and squabbling I want to. I don't want to absorb any more of anybody's petty little problems or cushion anyone from any more trifling troubles.

And I'm tired of saying, "Excuse me," and "No, don't bother," and, "It's no trouble." It *is* trouble, and they *ought* to bother, and they should be asking *my* pardon, not I theirs! They gather in front of the television set like moths around a light bulb, and to get across the den is to thread a complicated, giant-sized sewing machine. And they're all so *oblivious!*

That's the worst part, Lord. They're not even aware that somebody is going around the place doing all the night things: feeding the pets, bathing the baby, pulling the car in, locking up the house, adjusting the heat, putting out fresh linens. Who do they think does all these things, anyway?

All right. I've said enough. Better You should hear it than they, I suppose, Lord. Thank You for being *my* sponge and absorbing all *my* trifles and gripes and loving me still. I take shame to myself for my attitude. Teach me to love serving.

And thank You for loving me, Father. I love You—*and* them.

4
Secret Sins

It is disconcerting to me that the sins I find easiest to confess are those which I commit in public and which I judge (accurately, without a doubt) to make me look foolish. If I say something harsh or unkind or something with a double meaning, or if I do something in someone else's presence that I think would disappoint Christ, it gets on my conscience and stays there until I'm miserable. The fact that another human being has witnessed my sin lends it a heavy black outline in my mind, and I simply cannot live with it—or, rather, with myself—until I'm rid of it.

Would that I could develop the consciousness of God's Presence to that degree! To speak and act in unchristian ways is certainly to be repented of and confessed; is to think unchristian thoughts any less reprehensible? Not if we take Jesus' words in Matthew 5 seriously. I am convinced that the sins most damaging to my Christian growth and well-being and, yes, even to my Christian witness, are not those that I commit verbally or actively. Those that wreak the greatest havoc are those that take place in my mind. Thoughts of anger and spite, of covetousness and lust, of resentment and jealousy are corrosive to the spirit. My prayer life has been at times debilitated to such an extent by my thought-life that I retreat to a form-keeping routine of Bible and related reading that does nothing for my spiritual state. I simply try to keep the door open, but perhaps don't succeed even at that, because I am sure that at such times I am effectively closing God out and holding Him at arm's length.

The effects of sin in the thought-life are the more damaging because they work subtly and secretly to do their hurt. Sometimes I am unaware of the strength a thought-sin has gained until it springs to life in the form of a word or a deed, and then the harm is no longer mine alone to contend with; it is multiplied and set loose with infinitely more serious and widespread consequences. The family suffers, particularly my children; or friends are wounded needlessly; or, perhaps worst of all, a younger or newer Christian is deflected from the straight path by my leading. Then woe be unto me, for truly I deserve a millstone.

> God be in my head,
> And in my understanding;
> God be in mine eyes,
> And in my looking;
> God be in my mouth
> And in my speaking;
> God be in my heart,
> And in my thinking;
> God be at my end and at my departing.

5
For This Friend I Give Thanks

O, dear Father, I am grateful for many people who have been a part of my life. You have provided me with godly parents, a loving family, a dedicated husband, and a host of Christian brothers and sisters.

But, Lord, You did a special thing for me when you sent this friend who thinks I am good. She hasn't realized that I am often selfish, always self-centered. She won't recognize that I covet, I despair, I lust, I am proud and stiff-necked, I get angry and discouraged—or perhaps she knows this and looks beyond it. She knows me, and yet she sees me as an unselfish, giving, loving, joyous person.

Father, I thank You for that in her. I thank You that she sees in me what, perhaps, You saw in us all when you gave Your Son. And, knowing that she thinks of me as this kind of person, Father, I try a little more conscientiously to *be* that person. She is a daily reminder of Your hopes for me and of Your Presence in my life.

Truly I am blessed with this friend. Thank You, Father. Thank You.

6

Prayer for a Couple on Their Wedding Day

Oh, Father God, Source of all love, look upon these Thy children and grant blessing. Bind them together in a union which will never be disrupted as long as their earthly lives last.

Guide them during their first few days together so that the foundation they lay for their home will be based upon the Rock and therefore firm and sturdy. May their every decision be within Thy will for their lives. In every effort they make toward establishing their place together in this world, let Thy Spirit guide.

Help them to learn forgiveness early, for verily they will need it. Equip each with tolerance for the other's foibles, acceptance of the other's failings, and a sense of humor to see them through the disagreements and misunderstandings without which no couple ever built a home.

Grant that the love and laughter of little children may brighten their lives. Let their home become a blessing and a strength to friend and neighbor and a channel of divine love which will permeate whatever community they may live in. Lead them ever in paths of service which will help spread Thy Kingdom here on earth.

Remind them, O God, that the days of mortal love are short and to be cherished. Keep them ever aware of Thy love for them so that, though their life together on earth will one day end, they may continue an unbroken fellowship with Thee.

7
Seventy At Seventeen

O, Lord, Thou knowest that I love Thee. Thou knowest that I love this boy-man, this creature of Thine and mine who sits at the wheel of this conveyance.

Thou knowest, Lord, that I trust Thee. And Thou art aware that I trust this creature of ours—most of the time. But, lo, O Lord, Thou seest that when he drives a car, he is a new creature —not altogether mine, nor, perhaps, Thine.

Thou knowest that he and I do not see eye to eye here and now. He wants speed; I want safety. He seeks thrills; I yearn for serenity. He glories in his power; I cower in my seat.

But, Lord, I would not have him a boy always. Truly he needs my confidence in this, as in other things. How can he grow in skill and how can I grow in confidence but by the practice of each? So let us rehearse, both Act I and Act II.

My life is in his hands, Lord, but my soul is in Thine. I rest.

8
My Caution Light
Is Flashing Again

God, you know there are times when that kid scares me to death. He tells me with no little degree of arrogance that he can make his own choices and cut his own swath, and he doesn't need me around "making noises like a mother."

But, Lord, what kind of noises can I make? Whence but from You this concern, this aching, reaching pain in me when I see him make a foolish decision and hear him speak with so little thought? Am I, in truth, a worrier and a nagger as he accuses me, or didn't You put this extra caution within me because he has so little? Is it built into the relationship that my love comes across to him as a net effectively denying him his freedom? And I do love him, Lord; in our better moments I even like him.

I don't want to call a screeching halt to his headlong plunge into life. But somebody needs to put up the caution lights and the YIELD signs before him. Help me, Lord, not to be the big, red STOP sign in his life. Make of me, instead, a speed break so that just once on occasion he can slow down enough to look around him and get his bearings.

9
Prayer for a Thirteen-Year-Old

O, God, You love this little girl as much as I do. More, even —though that's hard for me to comprehend.

But she's not really a little girl any more, is she, Lord? Yesterday she was a gangling, knobby-kneed tomboy helping to build the treehouse. Today she is blossoming into womanhood, trembling with life and in love with it.

It's all ahead of her, Lord. She's got it all to look forward to. I wish I could take her by the hand and lead her around the hazards and hold her up when she stumbles, but I can't do it. I see it all there waiting for her, but she has to find it for herself.

She will learn something of the perfidy of women, self-serving creatures that we are; but she will also learn that a woman's friendship can be as deep-moving and strong as a mighty river and can carry her as far. She might discover that a man can betray and speak faithlessly, but I pray that she will also know the completing and fulfilling joy that a good marriage can bring.

One of the toughest lessons she will learn, Lord, is that she can't always trust herself. She doesn't know how she will react to a touch, a glance, a word. Grant that she will face no temptations too great for her to resist. Plant deep within her the shield of your Spirit. I would keep her innocent and ignorant of wickedness, Father; that being impossible, will You please build a firebreak around her so that she won't get too painfully burned?

10
Now He's Six

God, do You see this little one—this last one—kicking that stone out of his way as he strides off to first grade? How did he get to be six years old in such a short span of time? What did I do with those years, all those days we had together, the thousands of hours I spent with him?

Up to now he has been mine, Lord, and I haven't worried unduly about him. I've known his whereabouts and his companions and—to a large extent—I've controlled the atmosphere to which he has been exposed. I've overseen his activities. I pulled him and his tricycle out of the street; I helped him down from the branch that suddenly seemed fearfully far from the ground when he looked down; I kept the kitchen knives and the insecticides out of his reach.

But, now, Lord, he's going where I can't go. Someone else will have to kiss the hurt away and put the Band-Aids on. Someone else will have to encourage him to drink his milk and to keep a stiff upper lip when he's disappointed. Someone else will have to remind him to be kind to the crippled children and not to laugh at others' mistakes.

But suppose no one else does it, Lord? There's a crowd of children in that classroom; suppose he gets lost in the shuffle? Will he be bold enough to ask when he doesn't understand, persistent enough to search when he doesn't know the answers? Will he be strong enough to be kind when the crowd is teasing someone else and to say no when the "let's play" is wrong?

Lord, I know I haven't done my best all the time; I suppose that explains these doubts. But can You please supplement my second-best? Will You fill in the gaps I've left? He's little; he's trusting; he's vulnerable. I would have him still trusting and vulnerable when he grows big, Lord. But I would have him strong, too—strong and sturdy.

You love him, Lord; and You're far wiser than I. I give him to You for keeps.

11
Tit for Tat

She was unkind and unfair to my child, Lord, and I am angry enough to strangle her. How can a grown woman speak in such terms to an adolescent? How can a mature adult behave in that unthinking, slashing, destructive manner toward a younger person? How can she justify seizing the psychological advantage any adult holds over a young person and wielding it so unfairly?

Yes, I am angry. I am wild, raging, *furious.* I am ready to plot revenge. I want her to be hurt just as much as she hurt him—nay, more, much more. I want an eye for an eye and a tooth for a tooth. I want justice to roll down like mighty waters—never mind about mercy.

Wait, Lord; what was that You once said about turning the other cheek? About not being angry with my brother? Does that go for sisters, too? Suddenly I remind myself of a mother tiger, yowling and baring her fangs because her cubs are threatened. I'm supposed to have a mind and a soul that separate me from the animals—I'm supposed to be made in *Your* image. More than that, I'm supposed to be Christ's disciple; I'm supposed to react in a Christlike manner. What kind of example am I setting for my children when they see me in this fury that chokes me with tears?

Ah, Lord, am I shaming You again? Forgive me; melt my anger and remold this seething energy into love. I remember those who hurt You, and You didn't fight back. Grant me that kind of spirit, Lord; put within me that which is larger than revenge and stronger than retribution. Fill me with Your own Spirit; of myself I can neither love nor forgive.

Yes, Lord; she *was* unkind and unfair. But whose sin is the greater—hers or mine?

12
Now Is the Hour

His teacher says he is a happy child, Lord, and I want to thank You for that. Of all the things I want him to be at this stage of his life, happy would have to come first. He is too young to know sin, and so he does not know the cleansing relief of forgiveness. He hasn't yet experienced the angry hurt of a broken relationship, and so he doesn't know the joy of reconciliation. But happy he can be and happy he is, and I am so very thankful for that.

Doubtless the time will come when he will have to wrestle with grief and evil. He certainly cannot mature without living through his portion of hurts. He will know the wrenching, tearing pain of losing someone he loves in death; he will be hurt by others and will learn how dearly forgiveness costs; he will hurt other people, and will know the anguish of remorse. He will fail and be ashamed and humiliated, and he will have to rise above it; he will succeed and be proud, and he must learn to cope with that.

Just now, though, he doesn't need to worry about a thing. He can be gloriously, nonchalantly carefree. He can be in love with the world and deliriously happy in it. Blessed is he and blessed are those who know him—especially his mother. Thank You for my son, Lord. Thank You for Your Son who lives in him now and strengthens him and prepares him for the days ahead. Thank You, God, that this happy child is Yours—and mine.

13
I'd Rather Say Yes

God, I thank You for giving me the backbone to put my foot down. I didn't want to do it; I would much rather have let the whole thing blow over. That would have been infinitely easier. I don't like scenes, and I approached this matter with my heart in my mouth. Basically, I am a coward; but I hope that, by Your grace, I am becoming a committed coward.

Your Word tells me that You chasten those You love; I can't, as a mother, justifiably do differently, can I? Love spends itself in lots of ways, doesn't it, Lord? Baking bread is a breeze; running up a new dress or a shirt is simple; taking the children on an outing is pure joy. All that is love. Reading stories and sharing problems and laughing at jokes are all easy to do; and they are love, too. But love is also saying *no* when they want to hear *yes;* and love is denying them something they want that I know wouldn't be good for them; and love is insisting on a certain behavior at times when their inclination is to do the opposite.

Without Your strength I can do nothing, Lord; I can certainly not undertake to raise these children and fit them for their roles in the world singlehandedly. Not even the two of us together can do that. And so I give thanks that You are before us and within us equipping us for the job. Truly You are our strength and our shield. And—at times like this—our backbone, too.

14
I Can See!

I used to be scared stiff of my grandfather. He was a stern and dominating patriarch who ruled his children—and theirs—with an iron hand, a flexible wrist, and a glinty eye. He was a strait-laced minister who loved the companionship of other men; and, though we children often heard him swap jokes and laugh heartily with them, he was not the sort of grandparent who held you on his knee and teased you and gave you the sugar from the bottom of his coffee cup.

My brother and I once made a rather lengthy automobile trip with Grandad and he—duty-conscious if not doting—tried sporadically to entertain us. At one point, driving on rain-wet highways well into the night, he slowed down to study an inter-section and recited, " 'Let me see,' said the blind man; but he never did see at all."

I remember studying Grandad's face in the half light of the car and wondering what response was expected of me. Should I laugh politely at his wit? or was I supposed to sympathize with the poor, pleading blind man?

Adult reflection assures me that this incident remained with me because Grandad had stepped out of what I considered to be his character. And that silly little fraction of an anecdote— if such it is—has become a password for me as I search in my preoccupied way for the salt in the refrigerator. Notwithstand-ing, I'm glad it made an impression on my subconscious. Be-cause, as I recently reread the story of blind Bartimaeus, I was struck as with thunder by the thought that Bartimaeus made the same plea. And, praise be to a compassionate Saviour, he did see!

And we, too, can see. Day by day, year by year, as we seek to grow in our commitment and we pray for the light of God's guidance on issues and decisions, the scales fall from our eyes and we can see! We are not left to wander in the darkness of our prejudices, our ignorance, our misplaced yearnings. "Show me. Let me see!" we pray. And He does. Every time, consistently, without fail, He does.

God of Light, we thank You for the promise that we do not have to live in the twilight areas where right and wrong are indistinguishable. Give us the humility to admit it when we do not know what to do, the persistence to seek the Truth in every part of life, and the grace to do Your will once we see it.

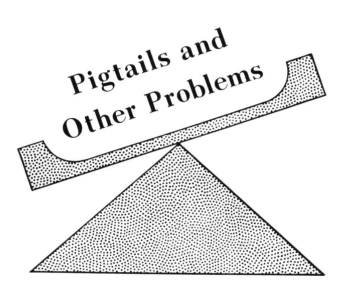
Pigtails and Other Problems

1
Watershed at the Water Fountain

I wonder if a conscious loss of innocence is a universal experience of childhood. A recurrent theme in Wordsworth's poetry is that the very young child, having come most recently from God, is most nearly like Him in motivation, purity, and goodness. And the further removed we become from that perfection of innocence, the more susceptible we are to corruption and selfishness. I leave the theology of that proposition for someone else to ponder. But I read some words in Revelation 2:4 that made me wish I could go back to the days before I hurt Elbert's feelings at the water fountain: "But I have this against you, that you have abandoned the love you had at first."

Elbert was the kid nobody liked. He wasn't included in our games—unless we needed him to even up the sides; nobody chose him to sit with when we did classwork in pairs; he wasn't well dressed; he walked in a slouch; and, on top of all that, he had buckteeth and about a million freckles. Naturally, he bore the brunt of most of the classroom jokes and teasing. Until the water-fountain incident, something of Elbert's lost-puppy quality had struck a chord in me, and I had—when it didn't cost me anything—done a kindness or two for him.

One day during recess I left a hot and fast game of some description and dashed inside the building for a drink of water. Elbert was there ahead of me relishing a long, cool draught. I waited impatiently. He took his time. Finally, with deliberate meanness and malice aforethought, I blurted out: "Hurry up, Freckle-face; other people are thirsty, too."

I can still see the unbelieving expression on Elbert's face when he looked up at me. For weeks after that, when the thought of him flitted across my mind, I felt a minor shock of something cold and unpleasant deep inside my being.

I wish I had not spoken unkindly to Elbert. I wish I had never abandoned the love I had at first. And I wish I could still feel the same degree of cold unpleasantness when I do or say something unkind and unloving and un-Christlike.

I wonder how Eve felt afterwards when she thought about that apple?

2
A Deep River to Cross

I've heard it said that the Lord protects those who can't protect themselves. I would add to that category those who are too foolish to do so.

My brother had an old fishing boat that he and his friends liked to use on the river which cut through our county a mile or two behind our house. Once when I was in my middle teens, he made arrangements to put in to the river at a point several miles north and fish down to a place I was familiar with; I was to take the car and meet him there at a certain time, give or take a half hour.

When the hour approached, I took my little sister and headed for the river. The rendezvous point had a beautiful sandbar, but it was on the back side of the river and one had to cross in a boat in order to enjoy it. The side which we could reach in the car was shady and marshy and snaky, the water deep and black at the bank.

We waited for the boys in the boat for a little while but soon grew restless. There is not a great lot for girls to do in a place like that, and the sandbar lay enticingly in view, white and clean in the sunshine—too inviting to resist. I untied somebody's old boat from a tree, found a splintery oar, put my sister in the other end of the boat, and set out for a good soak in the sun. My ignorance of currents and such being as complete as my disregard for the fact that neither of us could swim, I headed straight across the river, and we were scarcely halfway over when it became apparent that we would miss the sandbar entirely.

Sister panicked and jumped out of the boat and I—putting first things first for once—dived in after her. They say that drowning people view their past in a flash. I don't know about that; what flashed before my eyes were scenes of the imagined immediate future: dragging the river for my sister's nine-year-old body; explaining my brashness to my grieving parents; sleeping alone in the double bed I had shared with her.

The water was over her head but not over mine. I grabbed her in one hand and the boat in the other and dragged both to the sandbar. By the time the boys reached us, I had stopped trembling and had soaked up all the sunshine I wanted for a long time.

That night I lay awake for a short eternity, weeping with relief and thanking a heavenly Father for His protection. Many times since I have had occasion to be grateful for that same protection from hazards I did not have the good sense to foresee, not only physical, but spiritual and moral as well.

3
Lesson at the Clothesline

They say that the ideal educative method is to learn by doing. I believe it. The most graphic lessons I learned as a child are with me still, and most of them I learned by doing: something wrong. Like the day Mama washed her nylons.

The root of the whole problem was that I did not know how to appreciate nylon stockings. This must have happened towards the end or just after World War II, and I was far too young to realize the value—or the rarity—of a precious pair of nylons. I certainly wasn't aware that women guarded them with their lives nor that the fortunate soul who had a whole, unsnagged pair rated it on a par with her child: to be cherished, cared for, tended with loving, gentle hands.

One summer Monday morning I was roaming around the backyard looking for something to do when I happened to duck under the clothesline and was caressed by the long, filmy, just-dried leg of a nylon. It felt purely delicious—light, delicate, feathery. I turned around, got my directions, closed my eyes, and walked back under again and again in order to relive and relish the new sensation. But, as with repetition all thrills will, that one lost its zing and, pausing to analyze the source of my pleasure, I chanced to see a tiny, curly thread extending a quarter-inch or so at one point. It ruined the gossamer perfection of the tiny garment. *I'll just get that out of the way,* I said to myself. I got a tweezer grip on it between my thumb and forefinger and pulled carefully so as not to mess up any neighboring threads. Napoleon was not more horrified at Waterloo than was I when the entire lower half of that stocking dropped to the ground.

I put distance between myself and the clothesline, and Mama must have wondered whence the industry that cloaked me through the rest of that day and into the next.

I was thirty-one years old when I confessed this heinous crime to my mother. I hope she has forgiven me.

4
The Brat and I

We had the meanest boy in our sixth grade. He really was a toughie. Everyone knew his father "went off" periodically, though no one could say where. (Personally, I was sure that if son was like father, the old man was in the penitentiary during those absences, but that opinion was prejudicial.) At any rate, he could go places no one else our age was allowed to go; he turned up at school at the oddest hours; and some of us learned as much new vocabulary from him as we did from the teacher.

One day when school was out, I dashed alongside the building loaded with books, papers, and such, and that boy deliberately stuck his foot out and tripped me. My coat went in one direction, my books in another, and my lunch pail in a third. I sprawled full length and face down. Girls along about eleven or twelve are awfully conscious of Keeping Skirts Down and Acting Like a Lady, and my physical injuries that day were minimal compared to the damage to my dignity. Biting my lips and blinking back tears of fury and frustration, I scrambled around on my knees gathering up my things when, reaching for my coat, I suddenly locked eyes with Hal, also on his knees, also picking my things up. We stared at each other for a long moment, and then, with apology in every line of his body, he muttered, "Here's your coat," and turned his back and left. I sat back on my heels staring after him.

I think Hal and I both learned something that day. He must have discovered that his pleasure in playing tricks couldn't always balance the victim's humiliation. And I? Well, that was my first glimpse underneath a tough exterior; and I found that day, as I have many times since, a soft heart.

5
Milquetoast Was My Name

Along about the second and third grades, I was a part of a small group of congenial, busy little girls. We never wasted a minute together, progressing from work to play to school in uninterrupted accord. We piled up pine straw in the schoolyard and laid out elaborate houses complete with furniture. We played mamas and daddies, nurses and doctors, teachers and preachers, too. We had parades and church and funerals and weddings.

We were, at that age, rather frank about our shortcomings and strong points. One of the girls always acted as spokesman of the group; another was recognized as the strongest and when any activity required unusual physical prowess or dexterity, she paved the way for the rest of us. One was invariably a leader; others just as faithfully followers.

I remember the day we got into a session of nicknaming. We had Laughing Lucy and Small Sally and Muscley Marie (she was the strong one). One girl with a quick temper we named Mad-Too-Fast; she accepted it as fitting and smiled about it, as I recall.

I can still remember the sense of deflation I felt when nobody could think of a nickname that fitted me. There wasn't a thing about me that was special: not my size, my personality, nor my looks. I think I came away from that session feeling somewhat like milk toast: bland and tasteless, nothing you could get your teeth into. I had an urge to climb the flagpole, to stand on my head in class, to turn cartwheels across the lawn—anything to make people look at me and see that I was indeed—if they would just recognize it—*remarkable.*

It took me a long time to learn that I didn't have to be brilliant or beautiful or brave in order to be loved and cherished, to be something special. I did the adult equivalent of turning cart-wheels and climbing flagpoles countless times before I learned that I am uniquely, specially a child of God. Because He made me, I am worthwhile. Because He loves me, I am valuable. Praise be to a Father to whom even milk toast is flavorful!

6
Sister's Thistle

I always did have a flair for the dramatic. Apparently the safe, sane, rural existence provided by my parents was too sedate for my thrill-hungry soul; at any rate, I sometimes embroidered the routine and embellished the commonplace to make living more interesting. In my fertile imagination, a sprained ankle could become a broken leg which necessitated weeks in a wheelchair, followed by months on crutches, during which time I would, naturally, be noble and brave in my suffering, leaving a lifelong impression on lesser mortals around me. The first *C* on my report card (in deportment, to my everlasting shame) became the first warning sign that I was headed down the path of disgrace to family and degradation to self. Misunderstood and miserable, I would wander from pillar to post, from bad to worse, ever seeking the elusive *grande cause* which would set my heart afire and awaken the dormant shreds of fortitude and integrity within my bosom.

One afternoon three or four of us were engaged in some variation of hide and seek, and it came time for me to be *It*. I closed my eyes and counted until I got tired, shouted, "Ready or not—here I come," and darted purposefully toward the plum orchard. Halfway there I was frozen to my path by unearthly howls from the opposite direction. My sister! My adored older sister—the one who defended me in sibling warfare—who spoke up for me when a wrathful parent was on my trail—the one who never griped when I read over her shoulder—my sister was in trouble! And serious trouble, from the sound of it. The shrieks continued for a long minute, and then abated slightly. I did not know at that time what I learned during the first months of motherhood: the fundamental, step-saving principle of rearing a family is that the louder the child's howls the less likely he is to be in real need of assistance. I hastened to Sister's side, a lump of fear rising higher and higher in my throat. She was being attacked by a wild animal (a rabbit, perchance?); she had stumbled into a gopher hole and broken both legs (amputation might be indicated!); a snake (poisonous, no question) had bitten her!

Chagrin is not strong enough to describe the letdown I suffered when I came upon my sister sitting on a thistle. Nobody who did anything so unromantic deserved my sympathy. But I wonder how many times since then I have created a fatal snakebite out of a thistle prickle?

7
Mothers and Measles

When I used to read the words "my sainted mother," the phrase created in my mind a picture of a mild-mannered little old lady who wore a long, black dress with white lace around the neck. She sat in a rocking chair with her hands folded sedately in her lap and a beatific smile on her face, and she assuredly never spoke above a murmur. Now that picture doesn't describe my own mother in any particular, except for the fact that she did, on occasion, wear black. My mother was and is a vigorous, active woman with a multitude of interests and abilities to match; she wielded a needle, a trowel, and a paddle with equal skill and gusto.

I marvel that she is sane today. There must have been dozens of times when she could cheerfully have walked out of the house without a backward glance, leaving us to muddle along as best we could. That she didn't is a testimony to her Christian fortitude, not to her winsome offspring nor yet to her devoted husband.

Trouble never came in twos and threes at our house, usually in fives or sixes. I recall the summer we all had measles—not the three-day, hardly-know-you-have-it type, but the bad, old-fashioned sort that kept you thoroughly weakened and abed for at least two weeks. My brother missed the last day of school that year because he was sick; he stayed sick for two weeks, but nobody else got the measles—until his fourteenth day. My sister was second and I was third. None of us had the foresight or the kindness to join another in his wretchedness and thus shorten the ordeal for my mother; each had to have his day of glory, and, one by one, throughout that long, hot summer, the six of us endured the measles.

One afternoon during what must have been my second week

I had asked for a drink of water and, thinking to save Mama a few steps (I like to think that was my motive, but I was probably just tired of the bed), I got up to return the empty glass to the kitchen. The drain was full of clean dishes, and Mama was still at the sink washing up. I handed her the glass, and then, to my utter horror, the water and whatever else I had eaten rushed up and out and effectively showered the clean dishes.

My mother never said a word. She simply turned me around, guided me by the shoulder back to my bed, and mopped my face with a cool cloth.

Saints don't withdraw from the world and contemplate goodness from a rocking chair. Saints, among other things, raise children and retain their sanity—and their smiles.

8
Pigtails and Patience

I suppose every red-blooded American girl since Pocahontas has worn pigtails at one time or another. I did. For the first three or four years of school, my hair was nothing if not neat. Every morning, I sallied forth and faced the world and all that is therein with aplomb, secure in the knowledge that I was (for a little while, at least,) clean, pressed, and spiffy. My braids marched down either side of my head like twin railroad tracks, ending with two healthy handles bouncing back and forth over my shoulders.

And handles they were. There must be a special sort of frustration hidden in the breast of every small boy that is released simultaneously with the grasping of a pair of feminine pigtails. Certainly few of them resist the temptation. Beginning with my brother, not a male below the age of twenty with whom I had even a nodding acquaintance came near me without grabbing and pulling. I never rode a horse in my life, but I learned early the meanings of *Gee* and *Haw*. Schoolboys in my day could think up as many devilish things to do with pigtails as with rubber bands, paper clips, and peashooters. Many—yea, countless—are the times I have been called upon to recite and, attempting to rise, discovered that I was anchored to my desk. And, failing to tie these appendages to something else, a boy could always tie them to each other, along with pieces of twigs, cellophane tape, dead insects, and what have you.

I lived for the day when the scissors would release me from the bondage of pigtails. Freedom was never so sweet, nor yet sheep so blatantly, nakedly shorn as when Mama finally cut them off. I felt conspicuous, giddy, and wholly grown-up.

Not until I had a daughter of my own with her supply of snaps to replace, buttonholes to mend, and hems to put back in did

I appreciate the way my mother took care of me. She must have used a full ten minutes of an already busy, hectic morning schedule to put my hair in place. Not for her the quick and easy plaiting of a free-swinging mane; she did me up in French braids, and any woman knows that demands infinitely more patience and time.

For years the embodiment of teasing and torment, my pigtails have become the symbol of a mother's endless care and patience with a rapscallion, harum-scarum child. Funny how some lessons are taught so many years before they are learned!

9
The Mad, Mad, Mad, Mad Hatter

Our budding Thespian, age eleven, was chosen to play the Mad Hatter in the sixth-grade production of *Alice in Wonderland.* For weeks, we coached him in his lines, reading alternately the parts of Alice, the Queen, the White Rabbit, and others. He became letter perfect. He could and did say his lines in his sleep. But I fretted that he did not project his voice as he should. Suddenly, in the space of two weeks, this one of whom I had frequently said, "He has no conversational tone of voice," and whom I had cautioned times without number to "Keep your voice down, Son"—this circus barker who never whispered when he could speak nor spoke when he could shout could not be heard from a distance of ten feet. He kept saying, "Don't worry, Mom; I'll do okay," but, in the time-honored tradition of mothers the world over, I continued to fret and fuss and worry.

The big day was drawing near when he breezed into the kitchen after school one afternoon with the report that the teacher would like the costume to be ready a day early for the dress rehearsal.

"Costume?" I questioned in near panic. "What kind of costume?"

"Just so it has a hat," he told me. "Preferably a big hat. Or a funny one. Or a big, funny one."

I threw an inquiring glance at the head of the household.

"Don't look at me like that," he protested. "My hats are not funny, and, besides, they'd be too big for him."

Dad was entirely right. The smallest one rested on the bridge of our would-be Hatter's nose, and, while it looked funny enough to us, we thought that might not be what the teacher had in mind.

A canvass of the department stores turned up a couple of empty hat boxes. With scissors, cellophane tape, glue, and crepe paper, Dad set to work, and within a couple of hours turned out a top hat reminiscent of A. Lincoln. An outgrown coat of Dad's, with some judicious tucking and pinning, made a passable set of tails, and Sunday trousers completed the costume.

Zero hour was upon us. We took our seats and tried to look calm and nonchalant. A ripple of laughter and a wave of light applause greeted his first entrance onto the stage. His words rang out, clear and distinct enough to be heard in the last row. He seemed perfectly at ease.

At a particularly eloquent "Tsk! Tsk!" I looked at his dad. We exchanged a conspiratorial smile. A relieved smile. A happy smile.

Actually, what it was—was proud.

10
Sideline Scenario

I am convinced that neither doctor nor clergyman nor yet teacher can know a parent as well as a Little League coach or swimming teacher does. In the doctor's office, a parent is admittedly in the presence of one to whom, by training and experience, he is vastly inferior. It is a rare parent—no matter how worried nor how doting—who undertakes to argue with a doctor's diagnosis at the expense of his child's health. So the typical parent in the typical doctor's office is meek, submissive, and agreeable. And we all know we're on our best behavior in the presence of the preacher. Were he to take us at surface value, the average minister would think he preaches to a congregation of saints, noble, soft-spoken, and unfailingly pleasant. Now the school teacher possibly sees us in a less rosy glow as she explains why Johnny can't rule her classroom as he does his home, or why Rosie's quiet, attentive deportment does not necessarily mean she is learning anything.

But even the teacher, in her structured situation and with the authority of the city fathers presumably supporting her, does not see us at our abandoned, uninhibited worst. For the tiger in the parent does not really come out on display until the offspring is placed in an overtly competitive situation. At teeball and swimming, unlike the worlds of medicine and academics (not to say religion), every papa is a pro and every mother an expert not to be intimidated by any mere coach.

Here is the swimming instructor saying, "Put your face in the water; I want to see you blow some bubbles," while Mommy on the sidelines is yelling, "Keep your head up, Jennie! Keep your head up!" Poor Jennie, predictably overcome by fear and confusion, splashes like an angry cat and swims about as well. Or the coach is concerned with style and stroke while the parent reiterates over and over, "Speed is the thing. What we want you to do is *get there first!*"

I wonder if there is a baseball coach in the country who does his job unadvised and unaided by parents. From, "Be a hitter, son!" which isn't too bad, to "Don't you dare miss that ball!" leaving the poor little guy less leeway than the president has at a summit conference, a Little League baseball game is one long exercise in uncoordinated team teaching. One night I saw an earnest junior slugger step up to bat, wipe his hands on his pants, crouch in his best Babe Ruth stance, and, hearing his paternal voice of authority from somewhere behind him, look back to inquire respectfully, "Sir?" just as the ball knocked the bat out of his hand.

Oh, well, it's probably good practice for us all. Today's mommy who learns to stifle her comments will make tomorrow's ideal mother-in-law. And if a doting father can realize that missing a few hits won't ruin an entire season, perhaps he can let the boy make a few mistakes of other kinds later on without visualizing his complete downfall. And that's the way boys become men.

11
Worst Foot Forward

I don't suppose there is a girl in the world who approached her prospective parents-in-law for the first time without a certain amount of fear and trepidation. If there is, I should like to meet her. My own such experience was probably fairly typical, though it seemed to me at the time that the combination of excitement, anticipation, dread, and nervousness-bordering-on-illness which I was enduring had to be unique.

We had chosen the Christmas holidays to exchange visits with our respective families. My fiancé had made a hit with my parents, and his visit to our home was (with one little exception) a noteworthy success. He had a pair of elastic-waisted, baggy trousers that he enjoyed puttering about in and was wearing them on a day when we planned to visit a certain very proper aunt of mine. He had his first collision with my dad's dry humor when he asked him whether he needed to dress for the occasion.

"Well, no," was Dad's reply, "but I do believe I'd change from those pajamas you're wearing."

That visit completed, we headed north on the three-hundred-mile trek to his own parents' home, and my self-confidence diminished with every mile. Five minutes away from our destination I discovered a run in my stocking. Any woman knows what that circumstance does to the ego! But we were warmly welcomed, and if anyone wondered why I insisted on standing with my back close to the wall, he was too polite to say so.

A meal was already on the table, and though I have forgotten everything else about that dinner, I recall distinctly that the main course was pheasant. I had never eaten pheasant before; my reading had led me to believe it was something very wealthy English people ate under glass. I didn't even know the bird was native to North America. There was no glass in evidence (except those containing water), and I wondered whether my fiancé's mother had failed to serve it properly because she didn't want to seem pretentious to a simple, unsophisticated southern girl. (The years have since taught me that my mother-in-law is incapable of pretense. Her graces—and they are many—are as natural and as essentially a part of her as her hands.)

Never was a bride more sincere in her first efforts to please a set of in-laws. And if I did not do many wrong things, I did do many things unnecessarily and awkwardly. I left my purse at one aunt's house in a neighboring town, necessitating a twenty-mile doubleback at 11:00 P.M. (My father-in-law made great strides in patience that night. No matter what he thought—and I have never had the courage to ask him—he said nothing.) On an afternoon when guests were expected for dinner, my mother-in-law thrust a bunch of flowers into my hands with the suggestion that I arrange them for the table; she might just as well have handed me a Greek recipe and said, "Here, make this cake."

But I stuck the flowers in a vase and tried not to leave any more belongings scattered among the relatives. If I made many mistakes the family was mercifully silent about them or, in the case of my father-in-law, treated them with humor. And when, three years later, we presented them with their first grandchild —and a boy at that—they reacted exactly the way grandparents the world over are supposed to react.

Then I knew that I was over the hump.

12
The Red-Dot Lady

I love to be in my mother-in-law's kitchen when she's working in there. Over the years since my marriage, I have learned much of value: some insights gained from our conversations on every subject under the sun, including her son; some fascinating sidelights of family history which I could have learned nowhere else; some invaluable advice, the bulk of which—to her credit—I specifically asked for.

Many are the times I have dawdled over drying the silver because I wanted to hear more of what she had to say about something. She has a way of seeing things from the long view, whereas I stand so close to a problem I can't see any way around or through it. She has an empathy for teen-agers that is astounding to her children and gratifying to her grandchildren, and her understanding of preschoolers is exceeded only by her patience with them.

She never hustles and bustles busily about, but she can accomplish a remarkable amount in a short time. Like Cordelia's, her voice is "ever soft, gentle, and low"; in twenty-odd years of intimate relationship, I have never once heard her raise her voice in impatience to scold or argue. She carries with her wherever she goes an atmosphere of quiet and calm and peace.

There is a family anecdote which tells everything about her, and I know it is true because I joined the family while the job was still incomplete. It seems the new kitchen wallpaper had been ordered from a sample design which featured pea-sized red dots, but when the supply arrived the design was complete and exact except for the red dots. After the paper was hung, my mother-in-law, true to her nature both in patience and in the will to find a way, purchased a dozen or so bottles of bright red fingernail polish and proceeded to supply the dots that had been left off, at roughly four-inch intervals around the four walls. And her kitchen was not small.

She is self-controlled, but utterly compassionate. Her wit is the more delightful because it is unexpected from one so proper. She is never without a hankie when a child sneezes nor a diplomatic word when an adult is caught awkwardly in conversation. Her beauty is the kind that increases with each passing year.

In short, she is a marvel. I hope she knows how much I love her.

13
On My Honor

Mothers will consent to do a lot of things for the sakes of their children. I have found myself in some situations which made me wonder with good reason not only how I got there but—more to the point—how I was going to get out. I have been the guinea pig who endured the teen-agers' first trial runs behind the wheel on the highway (I stand in no awe of any driving instructor; *he* has his personal set of brakes). In the interest of togetherness, I have banged away at the piano between a trumpet in one ear and a flute in the other (the second thousand hours entirely justified the first). I have relearned my French verbs during many sessions of hearing conjugations; and I've had mini-midnight-refresher courses in everything from American History to Argentine Flora and Fauna.

But nowhere have I learned as much in as many different ways about as many things as I did during my term as a Girl Scout leader. In defense of the girls and their lack of progress, not to say downright regression, they did not have professional leadership that year. The kind thing to say is that I was out of my element; the *truth* is that, to a girl, those twenty-four scouts outstripped me in every project.

Thirteen scouts earned their skating badges that season; when I last tried roller skating, I fell more times than a toddler during his first month of walking. They had their toasting forks made and had emptied the marshmallow bag while I was still trying to persuade a tree to part with one scraggly twig. By the time we were ready to hike, I had learned my lesson and very prudently suggested that, since someone needed to remain at camp to check off requirements as the girls came in, I would be that one.

My colleague and I were the blind leading the blind. When

she very nearly stepped on a snake during one outing, she jumped high enough to qualify for the Olympics, and her screech could have been heard in the next county. Only the fun she poked at herself saved her from permanent disgrace in the eyes of our charges.

"Observe how coolly and calmly I faced that emergency, girls," she grinned. "Notice my immediate decision to jump away from, rather than toward, the snake. In this regard, if in no other, you will always be safe in following my example."

At the end of the season, one girl succinctly, albeit unintentionally, summed up the year's experience with one remark.

"I'm glad I'm moving up to Mrs. Roberts's group next year," she said. "I'm going to sign up for the Survival Course."

14
A Bristling Question

Within the breast of every man there lurks, I am sure, a desire to sport a mustache or beard or both. Whether an individual male succumbs to the temptation seems to depend upon several things: professional pressures, social acceptance (or lack thereof), physical comfort (I understand the first few days are one big itch), and perhaps wifely approbation.

We had a round of flu at our house, and the head of the family lay for about four days caring little whether he shaved, bathed, or even ate. On the fifth day, a bleary-eyed, grizzly epitome of the Morning After staggered into the bathroom and beheld himself in the mirror. *"Hm-m-mm,"* he muttered, as visions of the patriarchs and the founding fathers danced in his head. "Ah-*ha*," he pronounced, thinking no doubt of Magellan, Columbus, Marco Polo, and other worthies.

He advanced to the kitchen, one hand caressing his jaw.

"Honey," he ventured, "what would you think if I trimmed this thing up and just, uh, let it grow for a while?"

I opened my mouth to answer and, as luck would have it, his eye fell on the headlines of the local paper: COUNTY GOVERNMENT SETS CENTENNIAL, they proclaimed, and, in smaller type, HIRSUTE ADORNMENT YOUR TICKET TO FOLLIES. Never one to waste words on empty air, I closed my mouth.

To a man, our citizens laid aside their razors. Strops hung unneeded; spray cans clogged from disuse; the local barber went broke; and five wives bought new fur coats (Retribution Raccoon, we called it). There was a rush on king-size beds. The local gift shop laid in a supply of pipes, and every neighborhood sprouted at least one new professorial type.

One night, weary of trying to dodge embraces diplomatically, I dressed in my sheerest, shortest nightie, conjured up a devil in my eye, and slunk into the bedroom. Laying my toothbruth across my upper lip, bristles out, I murmured,

"Kiss me, my sweet."

He shaved in two minutes flat.

15
Marriage—Who Comes First?

Everybody needs to be first with somebody. One of the essentials of our makeup is that we feel necessary to someone else. We need to be assured that there is someone to whom we are supremely important: someone whose life would have a hollow space if we did not fill it, and whose days would lose some of their shine if we were not around.

The disastrous divorce rate in our country is a matter for national shame. And a matter for perhaps still greater sorrow is the fact that many couples—even Christians—who still share bed and board have lost the grip of essential caring that first made their relationship vital. Some who are parties to this kind of deadly dull marriage would be hard put to it to say where the relationship went wrong or what the missing essential is. I am convinced that many husbands and wives fail to build a real marriage not because of insurmountable financial problems, or disagreements about rearing the children, or difficulties concerning sex or the in-laws, or even that catch-all, incompatibility. Look around you at the couples you know who have faced one or more of these problems, sometimes simultaneously, and who survived them to enjoy a livelier, healthier relationship than was theirs in easier times.

No, I have an idea that many marriages wither on the vine because one partner failed to convince the other that he was the number one priority in her life. At some point another concern took on out-size proportions, or a multitude of varied activities sapped energy that should have been used to nurture the relationship, or the insidious disease of taking-for-granted crept in and wasn't recognized. And the pity is that the culprit is sometimes a busy involvement in entirely worthy activities— even in the church.

The teaching in Matthew 10, verse 37 and following, is difficult to understand. Jesus said that "He who loves father or mother . . . or son or daughter [or husband or wife] more than me is not worthy of me." It is true that we are to love God above all else and then each other. But our first and basic love for God ought to enhance and enlarge all our other loves. And I don't believe that a sound, stable, genuine love for God will ever make a marriage partner feel like a second-class citizen.

16
Signs of the Times

There are occasions when I think the more I say the less anybody hears. So from time to time I have resorted to tacking up a printed sign in a strategic place and practicing the art of silence.

My husband's mother did a masterful job of training him. I have never picked up stray socks or slippers, and he certainly is an easy man to feed, willing to try anything once. But with an expanding family and the resultant increase in laundry, I found that I was spending more time than I thought necessary closing snaps and zippers and turning garments right-side-out. My suggestions-turned-pleas being completely ignored, I hit upon a device which, after several years, continues to work beautifully. Above the laundry hamper, I tacked a sign with these words:

> If you would turn your shorts and shirts
> I would be so happy;
> And I would think my children had
> A very thoughtful pappy.

As the children grew older and learned to read, but became careless in their own turn, a shorter, more pointed message sufficed. ZIP THOSE ZIPPERS AND TURN THOSE SOCKS was displayed in bold, black letters in the children's bathroom until the day a certain male relative sheepishly inquired as to its explicit meaning and the identity of its intended readers.

A third bathroom notice has saved much maternal wear and tear. Placed where it cannot be missed, it suggests:

> If you would close the toilet seat,
> The bathroom would be clean and neat;

And I would avoid the stress and strain
Of dropping everything down the drain.

A tactful (and it is to be hoped), inspiring notice which has been on our refrigerator door for some months is not original with me. I found it in a book and typed it for the benefit of those who profess to watch their waistlines. It reads:

SELF-DISCIPLINE IS JUST AS SELF-SATISFYING AS SELF-INDULGENCE AND, IN THE LONG RUN, A LOT MORE RE-WARDING.

This suffices except when there is an unusually tempting goody in sight, and I have learned not to leave the fate of any such morsel to chance. Any pie or cake destined for a company meal or perhaps a neighbor's kitchen is usually labeled specifically: THIS IS FOR FRIDAY NIGHT. For the kindergarten crowd, I have found that a very large and prominent NO leaves no excuses but, even at that, temptation is likely to be too strong unless there is something else equally appetizing within sight.

There is, however, one practice I have left off entirely in recent months. For years, I slipped a loving, wifely note among my husband's belongings when he was to be out of town for several days. These usually took the form of a silly limerick or a one-liner such as, "Why aren't you at home in my bed where you belong?" tucked into a pajama shirt. But one of these tender missives fell accidentally into the hands of a gleeful relative, and I have not lived it down yet.

Henceforth, if he wants to hear from me when he is away, he can call me on the phone.

17
Science Lab Was Never Like This

My mother tried her best to rear her daughters with some housekeeping skills. That she was a miserable failure in my case at least was not really her fault. I have decided, after lengthy self-examination and in the hindsight provided by twenty years of struggling on my own, that I simply was not a very observant teen-ager.

For example, reason would tell you that any church-going female, especially one with a husband and children, who gets Sunday dinner to the table on time must have begun preparations Saturday afternoon. Or at least Sunday morning early. But that never occurred to me. For six months after we were married my patient bridegroom would come home from church, remove his necktie, read the newspaper, wander into the kitchen to peek under lids, pace the apartment, pick up a book, put it back down, stroll back to the kitchen—all this sprinkled periodically with, "Can't I help?" Finally one Saturday afternoon he suggested diplomatically, "Dear, why don't we have a sandwich and some soup tomorrow so you won't have so much to do when you're tired and hungry?"

I don't remember when I finally learned to plan and prepare a meal on time, but I do remember when I learned not to leave eggs boiling on a stove. We had spent a delightful week in the mountain home of a friend who was away visiting her children. We were preparing to leave, and I planned to pack a picnic lunch which we would stop to eat somewhere along the way. I put half a dozen eggs on the stove in a pan of water, and no one who knows me will be surprised to learn that my next action was to head for the Laundromat with a week's laundry —leaving the house empty.

No biology building at dissecting time, no industrial pollution, no amount of over-ripe fruit could equal the smell that greeted our noses when we returned. Oh, yes, he was with me—worse luck. We scraped and scrubbed, sprayed and mopped to very little avail. The spots disappeared, but the smell remained. Finally, having done all we knew to do, my husband set out to get a replacement for the pot, and I sat down with pen and paper to convey my abject apologies.

Our hostess reacted to the disaster with considerably better grace than did my spouse. She, in fact, thought the whole thing was funny. He did not.

All this happened ten years ago, and it has taken us that long to see the humor in the situation. I was relating the story recently to a friend and remarked that my husband was angry all the way from Asheville to Atlanta.

"Atlanta, nothing," he snorted. "That just happens to be where I regained a degree of self-control."

18
Staff of Life

With the passage of years I have developed (deservedly or otherwise) in my own family, at least, a reputation as a baker—not pies and cakes but bread. I have been fortunate enough to come along at a time when a return to the values of an earlier period seems desirable. The pioneering qualities of our forefathers (wonder why nobody ever speaks sentimentally of our foremothers?) are pointed out and encouraged and held in great respect. People with talents in candlemaking and tatting are in demand as group leaders and demonstrators. My husband's enthusiastic appreciation of the more fundamental skills of homemaking has been at once my despair and my spur toward greater things. I used to say that he was disappointed when he learned I did not make my own soap, but I think I regained his respect with my first successful loaf of bread.

Notice that I did not say my *first* loaf of bread. That loaf was an unqualified disaster, and if I had not had a strong stubborn streak I would have quit cold after that first try. In my typical impulsive, disorganized way I undertook to make bread one evening after supper when my husband was away at a meeting and I had nothing else to do. Things went well during the first steps of preliminary mixing, setting aside for half an hour, and kneading, and the smell that pervaded the house was nothing short of heavenly. The next step in the process was to "let rise until double." After thirty minutes or so, when there was no discernible swelling, I assumed the "rising" was a process which could take an indeterminate amount of time and, being sleepy, I closed up shop and went to bed.

Nothing in my experience had prepared me for the sight that assaulted my eyes when I entered the kitchen the next morning. Following directions to place the dough in a warm place,

I had set the bowl on a cookie sheet on a chair in front of the hot water heater. White goo trailed in elongated, elastic blobs over the bowl, onto and over the cookie sheet, likewise onto and over the chair, and finally to the floor, where it spread around water heater and chair legs alike. After I had finished crying, I cleaned up the mess, vowing all the while never to buy another package of yeast.

But the fragrance of that aborted loaf haunted me, and I progressed from total disaster to somewhat-of-a-mess to just-barely-edible. Fresh baked bread is still enough of a treat that any effort is received with acclaim. The children come in from school, sniff happily, and say, "Oh, boy, she made bread today." The man of the house breathes deeply, casts both arms heavenward, and pronounces, "Ah, woman, you've done it again."

All in all, I like being a pioneer woman.

Loosen Your Tension
and Operate
in a
Normal Manner

1
Loosen Your Tension

LOOSEN YOUR TENSION AND OPERATE IN A NORMAL MAN-
NER.

These words actually were a part of some sewing machine instructions I was studying, but they could just as well have been lifted from the pages of a *Growing Christian's Workbook*. Aren't they apt? The statement implies that to be tense is to be abnormal, functioning in a less than satisfactory manner. Some lay witnesses have an inelegant equivalent to these instructions, and we need to heed it: HANG LOOSE.

We begin our days with the sound of a strident, insistent alarm clock, and we end them with the "Ten O'clock News" (mostly bad). Into the hours between, we cram so many duties that we find it necessary not only to make a list, but to number the activities for priorities. That's the kind of world we live in, and each of us adds his own dab of color to the mural of confusion our collective society is painting. We don't need a new set of heart disease and ulcer statistics to remind us that our world is a tense and keyed-up one, peopled with tense and keyed-up beings.

But that way of living is neither normal nor Christian. Can you imagine Christ leaping into His chariot and making a mad eighty-miles-an-hour dash for Caesarea in order to get to a speaking engagement on time? Nor is it any easier to picture Him swallowing a couple of aspirin to combat a headache. We need to drink deeply of the well of peace He promised us: *Do not be anxious. . . . Martha, Martha, you are troubled. . . . Let not your heart be troubled. . . . My peace I give unto you. . . .*

I have long thought that to be in the Presence of the Man Jesus must have been a profoundly reassuring and soul-quieting experience. Conditioned by our pragmatic, technology-laden world, we want to see and hear and touch in order to understand and believe. But Christ knew us mighty well and warned us ahead of time. We *will* feel sorrow and travail, but "I will not leave you desolate; I will come to you" (John 14:18). We *will* be anxious and troubled, but Christ Himself is praying for us. Could anything in all creation be more strengthening than that knowledge?

O Source of peace, teach us to release our tension and operate in the normal, Christian manner.

2
Hurry! Hurry!

Our youngest yelled for more juice and, when I didn't move at the speed he wished, issued this imperious command: "Hurry! Hurry!"

My reaction, I suppose, was normal: I hurried but I was a trifle indignant that yet another had learned how to rush me along.

Later, however, I fell to mulling over that scene and its implications. What kind of atmosphere has developed in my home —indeed, what kind of world do we live in—that a child not yet two knows all about "Hurry! Hurry!"?

Now, I recognize that patience and flexibility are not virtues of the toddler. When he wants something, he wants it a few minutes ago; and the one who undertakes to persuade him to wait for it, or to change his mind about anything, needs cotton in his ears and the will of a dictator. But I had to admit to myself that this incident was all too typical of our way of living. In our neglect to put first things first, we dash from chores to church, from sewing machine to swimming pool, with nary a moment to consider why we do it and whether it's worthwhile.

"Be still, and know that I am God." I infer a condition here: *If* we will be still and quiet—*If* we will calm our harried minds and order our hurried days, then God can teach us about Himself. Confusion, uncertainty, the vague, troubled insecurity which plagues us can be replaced with assurance and peace. I never did learn much in a cluttered, noisy classroom; there was just too much competition for the teacher. Just so, I must straighten up my spiritual classroom and give the Teacher my undivided attention. I can learn; He is a competent Teacher. I can be still, and be sure.

Loving Father, slow us down. Call us to You frequently so that the foundation which must underlie all our living will be firm and solid.

3
Pebbles and Boulders

I had had a wretched day—one which made me feel, as a friend phrases it, "Like a milkshake—when everybody has a straw." One child had promised a cake for a bake sale but had failed to notify the cook—me. Another waited until the last minute to go to her closet, and then couldn't find "one single thing to wear that fits or feels good!" One of the little boys had a runny nose and the crankiness that goes with it. And, though I can't cite specifics just now, it is safe to say that the fourth member of the quartet had contributed his share of transgressions. When the phone rang late that afternoon and I recognized my husband's voice, my first impulse was to snap, "Don't you dare ask me to do a thing!"

For whatever kept me from it, I am thankful. But honesty compels me to admit that far too often my disposition hangs a black wreath around 1 Corinthians 13. One of the many questions I am saving to ask Saint Paul is whether he doesn't think love can just once on occasion be a trifle impatient and irritable? It has been a mystery to me that, faced with a difficulty almost too great to be borne, we Christians can hitch up our figurative britches and have at it with a will. I suppose adversity uncovers for us strengths we didn't know we had. On the other hand, the gnats and flies of everyday existence can nibble our reserve of Christian charity down to a raw nub.

The malady is fairly easy to diagnose—the cure easier to prescribe than to effect. Bombarded by husband-holding advice from secular magazines, caught up in the whirlwind of civic and social activities, utilizing every minute of time and every ounce of energy for laundry and meals, is it any wonder that we meet ourselves coming and don't like what we see?

Perhaps we need frequently to reread the Mary and Martha

story (it's in Luke 10). And perhaps the key word in Jesus' admonition to Martha is *chosen.* Mary had chosen the good portion. It is imperative that, having chosen Jesus as Lord, we now choose to spend with Him the time necessary to shore up our reserves of love and patience and kindness.

By necessity, most of us women are Mary and Martha, too. Martha's duties will get done—occasionally at the prescribed time—often somewhat tardily. But Mary's moments, once they have passed, will not be available again. We must choose the good portion, and act daily upon that choice.

Loving Father, we forget that You are as willing to help us with our pebbles as with our boulders. Forgive us for "saving" You for the big ones.

4
Steadfast Love

I am impressed with the number of times the word *steadfast* is used in the Scriptures to describe God's love. It is particularly frequent in the Psalms. When I read, "For steadfast love is before my eyes, and I walk in faithfulness to thee"(26:3) I am reminded of the kaleidoscope toys which fascinate my children and which I find intriguing myself. I am told they are structured with mirrors and colorful stones so that the formations, though they change, are symmetrical. On close observation, one can see that there is a spot which is constant; the patterns vary with each turn of the cylinder but there is always that point of reference from which the reflections spread identically.

It occurs to me that a man's life is something of a kaleidoscope-in-time. Whether we turn the cylinder ourselves or it is turned for us by circumstances or another creature, the shape of our lives is continually shifting into new and unanticipated patterns. The very stones upon which we have laid our foundations can crumble beneath us; talents, senses, even loves which we may have taken for granted for a lifetime may be with us one week and gone the next; the cliché about death and taxes being the only sure things may suddenly be a throbbing, terrifying reality.

But the real foundation stone doesn't crumble. I like that word *steadfast*. The dictionary defines it as "firm, fixed, . . . established; constant, not changing. . . ." This is the kind of God who gave us life and made it worthwhile; He is the one who knows every thought in our minds—and the reason for it. He knows us in despair, in futility, in sin; He understands every fear, every anxiety; not a wish crossing our minds escapes His perception. And yet He loves us with a *steadfast* love, and that love is at the center of our ever-changing patterns of life.

Through our hurts, our temptations, our testings we can discern the love which is the cornerstone upon which we build. Nothing can change it.

The majestic Ninetieth Psalm says it best:

> Lord, thou hast been our
> dwelling place
> in all generations.
> Before the mountains were brought
> forth,
> or ever thou hadst formed the
> earth and the world,
> from everlasting to everlasting
> thou art God.
>
>   Verses 1, 2

And right now, too.

5
Who Is a God Like Thee?

I recall the morning our Shakespeare professor introduced us to *Hamlet* with words something like this: "Students, literary scholars have exhausted *Macbeth; Romeo and Juliet* has been plumbed; *Othello* has been plumbed. But, young ladies, *Hamlet* is inexhaustible."

Though I agree that exploring the depths of Shakespeare's characters is an exhilarating activity, I do not know whether *Hamlet* is inexhaustible. I am sure, however, that when Paul spoke of the "unsearchable riches of Christ" he used the right words. No matter how long and close our acquaintance with God, we can only begin to suspect the magnitude of His love and mercy and gracious acceptance of us. To glimpse the profound grace of God toward us His children is surely to spend a moment in the Kingdom.

Strange the little oddments that open up these glimpses for us: the beatific smile of a child who has mastered a new task and looks to you for approval; the tiny, intricate formations of some small creature's discarded shell; a straightforward, searching gaze from a teen-ager who questions, in sincerity, some of your beliefs; the first chords from the organ on Sunday morning; the grasp of your mate's hand as you observe a sunset—or a son—together. Every good and perfect gift does, in truth, come from Him. And what a blessing to go to bed at night knowing that God has somehow expanded your soul a little bit; and tomorrow—if you let Him—He will find a way to do so even further.

And tomorrow . . . and tomorrow . . . and tomorrow. . . .

The prophet Micah asked, "Who is a God like thee, pardoning iniquity and passing over transgressions . . .? He does not retain his anger forever because he delights in steadfast love (7:18).

114

I hope I live to be ninety. And I hope, by the mercy of God, to learn something new about Him each day. And I know that, even then, there will still be depths of God's love which I will not have plumbed.

6
Mistakes I Have Made

My parents used to subscribe to *The Progressive Farmer.* In it there was a column called "Mistakes I Have Made" which, as an adolescent, I read as faithfully as any contemporary housewife reads Ann Landers. The column, as its title suggests, featured letters from readers who confessed to some action resulting from poor judgment. Sometimes they would relate how the mistake had been rectified; more often, as I recall, they lamented, "If only . . . !"

Men and women are fallible beings, prone to error. And if a commitment to Christ helps sort out the jumble of our motives, unfortunately it doesn't perfect our behavior. So Christians make mistakes; or—not to euphemize—we sin.

I suppose, if deterrents to growth in the Christian faith were recorded and catalogued, high up on the list would be the plague of unforgiven sin. I speak here not of unconfessed or unrepented sin, but of that for which we are heartily sorry, but whose burden we still carry. Christ forgave the woman taken in adultery, and Scripture does not imply that she disbelieved Him. He told the paralytic that his sins were forgiven, and the paralytic accepted the forgiveness and the healing which was its manifestation. Why are we so reluctant, then, to accept Christ's forgiveness? Why do we so rarely feel completely free of guilt?

Though we may at first scoff at the idea, we must come to admit that the inability or the refusal to accept forgiveness issues from pride. We think we are such special people that even our sins are special—and thus especially repulsive to God —and especially difficult to forgive. If you have a guilt hangover, think for a minute: Do you not think this sin is so much worse, or greater than most that no ordinary forgiveness will do?

Two things in my reading helped me at this point. Hebrews 10:19, in the Phillips translation, reads this way: "Where God grants remission of sin there can be no question of making further atonement." Forgiveness is immediate to confession, and it is a twisted pride which makes us clutch at our past sins and hug them to us. The second help, paraphrased from Dietrich Bonhoëffer's *Letters and Papers from Prison,* brings an almost comic relief: God does not find our mistakes a whole lot harder to deal with than what we consider to be our good deeds.

If we are surrendered to Him, we're not too big for Him to handle. Leave the job to Him.

O, God, prevent us from cluttering our spiritual attics with old sins, lest we drag them out and start playing "Remember when. . . ."

7
Wisdom

There is a verse in the Ninetieth Psalm that struck me anew recently and sent me on a search through the concordance to find out what the Bible teaches about wisdom. "So teach us to number our days that we may apply our hearts unto wisdom" (verse 12, KJV). These words had always conjured up in my mind a picture of a hoary-headed old fellow tottering towards the grave gathering up knowledge as fast as he could because he had only a few days left to go. But, a couple of verses later, I see these words: "Satisfy us in the morning with thy steadfast love that we may rejoice and be glad all our days" (verse 14). That doesn't sound like an old man, does it? Rather this prayer must have come from someone in the dawning of life, with the vista of years to come stretching out before him like a vast prairie to cross.

And it is truth, indeed, that we cannot make a successful crossing of that prairie without the godly wisdom the psalmist prayed for. It is not a head full of knowledge that we need but a heart full of wisdom, and they are two different entities altogether. Adolf Hitler may have been a genius intellectually but he was far from wise. It is probably safe to say that a single intelligent, unwise man in the grip of Satan can inflict more far-reaching, permanent pain on the world and its people than a whole covey of loutish, ill-intentioned dolts.

And those of us who consider that our motives are wholesome and good—well, we still keep the Lord busy forgiving us, don't we? Even good intentions—without a God-given, mitigating wisdom—will not keep us from sin. So we can't afford to wait until we have finished with our other work to retire from activity and go about the business of becoming wise. It is while we are in the world—raising our children, teaching in the church school, serving community needs, working at whatever is ours to work at—that we need the wisdom God promises. And the great blessing is that He *does* promise it: "If any of you lacks wisdom, let him ask God who gives to all men generously and without reproaching, and it will be given him" (James 1:5).

We need not plod our way through life bumbling and muddling about. We can live abundantly, victoriously, joyously, deciding and doing and being with a wisdom greater than our own. We can live above ourselves—in the realm of the Kingdom.

Father, in ourselves we are certainly not wise. We are foolish, struggling, straying children in need of help. You have promised, Lord, and now we ask. Give us wisdom, please.

8
Whatsoever State. . . .

Paul said, "I have learned in whatsoever state I am, therewith to be content" (Philippians 4:11 KJV). I have a strong suspicion he never found himself facing any of these situations:

An eight-dollar bottle of medicine, full except for one dose, emptied into the eye of the stove;

A half-can of Parmesan cheese in a toddler's head ten minutes before time to go to Sunday school;

A bottle of syrup turned over on an open cookbook;

Two pairs of very wet, very muddy small shoes coming in the kitchen door, and it not yet nine o'clock in the morning;

Three balls of yarn being used for pitch-and-catch by two little boys;

Two dozen homemade rolls waiting to be put into the oven —discovered with two dozen inch-deep finger-sized holes, one in the top of each roll;

Toothpaste oozing out of the almost-new tube, not from the top but through a mouth-shaped series of little holes in the side;

An intricate, original design of curlicues and squiggles extending the length of the hall carpet—executed with hand lotion;

Chewing gum visible anywhere, but especially in hair!

120

Nope; whatever my state of mind under these conditions, it certainly isn't contentment. Rather I feel like wailing with David: "How long wilt thou forget me, O Lord? for ever?" (Psalms 13:1 KJV).

9
Here to Stay

If my husband should ever—by some freak of democracy—get elected to the White House, he will have to be the first commuter president. I simply refuse to move again. I spend the first six months after every change in residence wishing I could revert in time to the days when people were born, grew up, married, and died without ever crossing county lines. The mobility of our century is, in my mind, not one of its more shining characteristics.

Actually, I have been happy everywhere we have lived, though it took a little longer to "settle in" at some places than at others. And there is enough of the child left in me to quicken with a certain amount of excitement and anticipation when a change is in the wind. But that doesn't entirely balance out the negative aspects—and they are many—of moving.

A phone call on Monday morning to see whether you are still ambulatory after a long, rugged weekend; another to say, "Put on the coffee pot; I'm coming over for a minute"; another one to ask, "Could you endure two more children for a couple of hours? Bob's got to check into the hospital for some tests"; and another that says, "Come on over; we just made ice cream." Familiar voices all, and dearly loved. From that, you move into a house whose creaks sound different, the hot and cold water faucets are switched and you scald yourself half a dozen times the first day, and if the phone rings at all it is someone to say he's coming out to check that filter your husband called about.

And the things you can lose and ruin! We spent two Christmases in one house and had to buy new decorations because we never did find the old ones. (They turned up in a dining room closet when we packed to move the next time.) We have misplaced children's clothes so long they outgrew them (but to be perfectly candid, I'm not sure those incidents were entirely accidental). And my sewing machine has never been the same since it toppled over and nestled between the deep freeze and the doghouse during one move.

I've heard people say that three moves equal a fire. There are times when I think we need a good, roaring bonfire to eliminate some of the excess baggage we carry around. When we married and moved to seminary, we carried all our earthly possessions (with the exception of wedding gifts of fine china, crystal, and so forth) in the back seat and the trunk of the car. The next move necessitated two trips in the car, and the third a small trailer; but I daresay that if my husband had dreamed he would ever have to endure such a move as our last, he would never have proposed.

We lived for fifteen years in furnished parsonages, and our personal possessions included such items as a lawn mower, a typewriter and table, and a small mountain of books. Then we bought a house—empty—and were faced with the alternatives of furnishing it or camping in it. A raid on family attics from Memphis to the Gulf Coast produced a skeletal inventory; a generous church member contributed some beds; and, not being particularly taken with the idea of eating on the floor, we bought a table and some chairs. The result is described to acquaintances as Eclectic and to friends as Recent Donation.

It took thousands of miles and hundreds of hours to get this collection to a central point, and, as in having a baby, the last day (which, as it happened, was our wedding anniversary) was the worst. At the end of it, staggering with fatigue, we bedded down the children, upended a packing crate, spread it with a dish towel, and sat down to a sandwich and a bottle of pop.

"Happy anniversary," I said, as I brushed away the last cookie crumb.

"May we never have another like it," he groaned. And he stretched out on the floor and went promptly to sleep.

10
There's a Place for Me

My husband is a teacher at heart, I have no doubt of it. He is never happier than when showing one of the children how to do something—riding a bike, throwing a ball, operating the lawn mower, making a kite—whatever the project, he is in his element as master to their apprentice.

All this is fine and appropriate at this stage of the game. But until these children came along, he had no one to teach except me, and as a pupil I am somewhat less amenable than they are. Many are the times I have wanted to fly in the face of his instructions and do something exactly the way he suggested not doing it because . . . well, I don't know why. Who needs a reason?

For example, for years he tried to persuade me to separate the wastepaper from the wet garbage in the kitchen. For the life of me, I can't see the sense of such a thing as it all goes into the same plastic bag to be picked up anyway. Or he predicts caustically as I stand on my head reaching into the darker confines of a closet, "One of these days you're going to open that door and nobody's ever going to see you again."

I didn't clean that particular closet until we moved away eighteen months later, and I still don't separate the wet garbage from the dry. But, truth to tell, most of his suggestions make sense. From the first day of our marriage to this, the single thought that has gone through my mind more often than any other has been, "Now why didn't I think of that first?"

Things reached a watershed one day when he favored me with some kindly suggestions on the various effective ways to clean a rug, none of which I was using. As fate would have it, his method removed a spot that had refused to budge for me. It was too much.

Later he found me in the bathroom drowning my sniffles with the sound of running water.

"I can't do anything right!" I wailed. "Nothing ever works right for me. You're always having to straighten out something for me. And I never know where I stand with you!"

He reached out one arm and hugged me to him.

"Right up against me—that's where," he pronounced.

And that took care of that.

11
Two Directions at Once

We saw the movie *Doctor Doolittle* and were amused by a rather distinctive animal, the two-headed pushmi-pullyu. The circus master chortled gleefully that he'd "never seen anything like it" in his life. But as the comical creature ambled across the screen, I thought to myself, *There goes the average Christian— headed in two directions at once.*

We make a decision of the mind, and we commit our souls to Christ's keeping, and we surrender—to the extent of our understanding—our wills to His. But, always and unceasingly, there is tugging at us and tempting us the pull of the world, the call of Satan, the influence of evil. Call it what we will, we are never free of it. Spiritually we are a bunch of pushmi-pullyus; though we may have only one head, we are manifestly of two minds, and the resultant tension is at once the despair and the growing edge of the conscientious Christian.

Paul, with his revealing honesty, said it for us: "Wretched man that I am! Who will deliver me from this body of death?" And, a little earlier, "I do not do what I want, but I do the very thing I hate" (Romans 7:15). So we know we are in good company; if such a stalwart Christian as Paul suffered this tension, we cannot expect to avoid it. But, as with other problems, recognition is not solution.

Nevertheless, Paul apparently did find a solution, and I have often wondered what experiences he had between the writing of those words in Romans 7 and these following in Philippians 3: " . . . one thing I do, forgetting what lies behind and straining forward to what lies ahead, I press on toward the goal for the prize of the upward call of God in Christ Jesus" (3:13,14). Here is obviously the key for any Christian. If we want to live in victory, we must forget the past—old sins, old temptations, pre-

vious hurts, past painful experiences of one sort or another—
and keep our eyes fastened on the goal we are aiming for: the
perfect will of God worked out in our lives. The more sin-
glemindedly we strive for that goal, the fainter will grow those
tempting calls from the world.

No man can achieve this goal of perfection through the mere
effort of his will; and I do not believe the answer is to wear
blinders or to withdraw from the workaday world. But it is
within our power to check our direction daily and allow God to
correct whatever variances may have crept in.

To look in one direction only is not easy, but it is both possible
and necessary. And, who's to say, if we keep to the path more
faithfully we might avoid some cricks in our spiritual necks!

O God, we hear many voices: calling, teasing, tempting,
bewildering, frightening voices. Tune us to Your call, and let
the others fall into their proper places in the perfect harmony
which only You can arrange.